WILD
FLOWERS
OF SOUTH AFRICA

APPROVED BY THE
NATIONAL BOTANICAL INSTITUTE, KIRSTENBOSCH

STRUIK

(Contents page): *Gloriosa superba:* Flame lily.

PUBLISHER'S NOTE

The Publisher wishes to thank the National Botanical Institute, Kirstenbosch, and its staff, especially Dr John Rourke, for their valuable advice and assistance in the compilation of this book. We also wish to acknowledge the expert opinions of Dr B.L. Burtt of Edinburgh and Dr O.M. Hilliard of Pietermaritzburg regarding the identification of certain of the plants illustrated.

Struik Publishers (Pty) Ltd
(a member of Struik New Holland Publishing (Pty) Ltd)
Cornelis Struik House
80 McKenzie Street
Cape Town 8001

Reg. No.: 54/00965/07

First published in hardcover 1980
First published in softcover 1987
Second edition 1996
4 6 8 10 9 7 5 3

Cover design by Abdul Amien
DTP Manager: Suzanne Fortescue
Design Assistant: Lellyn Creamer
Page layout by Deirdré Geldenhuys
Reproduction by cmyk Pre-press (Pty) Ltd, Cape Town
Printed and bound by Kyodo Printing Co.
(Singapore) Pte Ltd

ISBN 1 86825 897 1 (soft cover)

CONTENTS

A field of daisies along the West Coast.

INTRODUCTION

South Africa's native plant life — the richest temperate flora in the world — has been explored by botanists for more than three centuries, yet continues to yield previously unknown species so that the studies begun by men such as Thunberg and Masson continue today. Since the first specimens of South African plants were sent to Europe for identification, more than 24 500 taxa (species, subspecies and varieties) of flowering plants indigenous to this country have been discovered, though the figure will doubtless prove to be even higher.

Some are rare, many are prolific, and they range in habitat from the arid wastes of Namaqualand and the Karoo to the lush sub-tropical greenery of the Lowveld, from the dark coastal forest of the Outeniquas to the rugged peaks of the Drakensberg. All have an appeal, whether they are burnished spears of aloes dotting an Eastern Cape hillside, the lordly strelitzias necks proudly craned, the bashful disas or the foul-scented carrion flowers whose pungency attracts the flies which pollinate them.

From this vast botanical treasure-house some 350 of the best-loved species have been chosen for this book. The selection of these has been a daunting task, for to catalogue all our indigenous flowering plants would require 70 further books of a similar size to this — and even then such a 'library' could well be incomplete. It would prove an impossible undertaking both because of the sheer volume of physical work it would involve, and because professional botanists are, as yet, far from completing a descriptive enumeration of all the flora native to our country.

For the botanist, both professional and amateur, this partly uncharted realm provides an exciting challenge and while four-wheel-drive vehicles and modern photographic techniques have replaced the ox-wagons and sketch pads of Thunberg and Masson, many novelties are still to be found and new, undescribed species constantly come to light.

South African botany will continue to present an ever-expanding area of exploration for many years to come but it is clear that, in the foreseeable future, a complete guide to all South Africa's wild flowering plants is hardly feasible. At the best one can prise the door ajar and provide a glimpse of part of the incredible wonderland.

The photographs in this book show some of the better known, more colourful plant families that are distinctive of our country. They are arranged in a sequence that approximately follows Engler's system of classification, with the exception that, as a matter of convenience, the monocotyledons are placed before dicotyledons. In some cases detailed studies or well-illustrated publications are available dealing with certain plant groups which here are covered by only a few photographs. Those seeking further information are referred to the bibliography, whose specialist works would form a useful foundation for a botanical library.

Gazania krebsiana: Oranjegousblom

VELD TYPES

In most books on wild flowers, the plants are arranged in taxonomic order, that is in families, with species classified into genera, and genera into families, all arranged in such a manner as to reflect their supposed affinities. However, plant ecologists prefer to study species in distinctive associations or communities, for example in different types of forest, grassland or succulent scrub.

In South Africa the most useful category of plant association is the 'veld type', devised by the late John Acocks, one of the most brilliantly talented botanists this country has produced. He divided, described and mapped the vegetation of southern Africa into 70 veld types, and enthusiastic naturalists who travels the country by road would gain much pleasure and profit from carrying a copy of Acocks' book with them, and so observe the changing veld types they pass through.

Fynbos, that unique veld type in the South Western Cape mountains, is dominated by families like Ericaceae and Proteaceae, but also contains some endemic families — Bruniaceae and Penaeaceae — which have evolved there and nowhere else in the world. It is best enjoyed on long hikes through the Cedarberg, Hottentots Holland, Klein River, Riviersonderend, Langeberg and Outeniquas. Fynbos has no apparent dormant season — every day of the year something is in bloom. Its special richness is world renowned: moreover, three quarters of its component species are endemic!

Namaqualand, on the other hand, is legendary for it great spring displays of daisies, but these are brief, often erratic shows, dependent on good regular winter rains. Many visitors to Namaqualand expect to see white, orange or golden fields of *Ursinia*, *Arctotis*, *Dimorphotheca* or *Osteospermum*. These large daisy genera are perhaps the backbone of the whole spectacle, but the real delight of that strange wilderness lies in the discovery of countless small plants — bulbous species of the families Iridaceae and Liliaceae — found everywhere among the bushes and koppies, but often unnoticed amid the more blatant massed displays. Namaqualand is best visited from mid-August until late September, although if rains are regular and well-spaced, even October can provide a rewarding show. This is, above all, the place to get out of your car and walk in the veld and, more often than not, get down on your knees! Those who only view Namaqualand from the seats of a car miss its true botanical glory.

The KwaZulu-Natal Drakensberg must also be high on any flower-lover's list of places to visit. A summer rainfall region, it is brown, dry and frosted in winter. But summer brings lush green subalpine meadows alive with orchids, bulbs and perennials: and here again one must be on foot to see the best of the flora.

In a very different way the Lowveld and Bushveld in Mpumalanga have great botanical appeal. Here there are areas where South Africa's most magnificent trees are found. Not trees of great stature as in the Knysna forests, but trees with startling forms, brilliant flowers and singular fruits . . . Again, this is an area containing a considerable diversity of species. Indeed, the Kruger National Park should be visited if only to enjoy its marvellous arborescent flora.

Parts of the Southern Cape and Eastern Cape Province are also well worth visiting, for this area is the meeting place of many diverse veld types often found closely adjacent to each other. The Little Karoo, with its rich succulent flora, is only a few kilometres from the fynbos of the Outeniqua Mountains and the temperate evergreen forests of Knysna, while at the eastern end of the Langkloof, subtropical elements from the Eastern Cape bush start to appear. With Plettenberg Bay as a base, one can see a good cross-section of the country's floral diversity in a single day's drive.

FOLKLORE

South Africa's wild flowers have a scientific as well as an aesthetic appeal. While many wild plants are grown as ornamentals in our gardens — some have even been hybridized, selected and improved — the flora is also of great scientific interest. It is an intellectually stimulating exercise to study the relationships of plant species, how they have evolved, or how their biochemical systems operate.

But to the indigenous peoples of this region the flora is, largely, of utilitarian interest. Wild flowers may be pretty to look at . . . but their roots, berries or bulbs can often be eaten. Arrow poison can be prepared from the latex of others, spells or magic can be encouraged with certain leaves or roots, and there are few plant families that are not used for medicinal purposes by traditional healers.

CONSERVATION

In whatever field lies man's interest in the wild flowers of the sub-continent, it is a sad fact that South Africa's indigenous flora is disappearing at an alarming rate. Farming, urban development and other pressures on land use, each year account for extensive and irreparable destruction. Some veld types are under particularly serious threat, such the Cape Fynbos where a high proportion of its component species are now regarded as endangered. Fortunately, reserves are proclaimed from time to time and strict conservation legislation is enforced in all provinces, but even these measures can never be wholly successful. Conservation of flora ultimately depends on the public, on local and on individual interest, but can only be promoted by people who are adequately informed.

We hope that this book will open many eyes to the natural wonders on our doorsteps and so help to stimulate and increase an informed interest. Man depends on plant life for his very existence and the more South Africans can be persuaded to grasp this fundamental fact, the better will be their country for future generations.

A beautiful display of yellow Nieuwoudtville daisies.

Mimetes cucullatus and *Restio:* Rooistompie and reeds. (See page 38)

LILIACEAE

The Liliaceae form a large cosmopolitan plant family, very well represented in South Africa where over a thousand species occur, most of them highly ornamental. One of their features is that they are mainly either bulbous or rhizomatous, although succulent and even tree-like forms, as in the aloe, are widespread in this country.

Aloe, with over 140 species in South Africa, is the largest and best-known genus. They grow almost everywhere, brightening winter landscapes, often in brilliant massed displays. The medicinal properties of *Aloe ferox* have been known for a long time and Simon van der Stel found it to be an excellent purgative. Juice tapped from the fleshy leaves is collected, solidified to a crystalline form and still sold under the name, 'Cape Aloes'.

However, the Liliaceae are known chiefly for their horticultural importance. *Agapanthus*, *Kniphofia*, *Lachenalia* and *Bulbinella* are all South African genera which have been improved and hybridized and are now grown in gardens throughout the world.

Ornithogalum includes not only the famous white-flowered chincherinchee, *O. thyrsoides*, but also yellow and orange-coloured species. Most ornithogalums, of which there are about 60 in South Africa, are extremely poisonous to stock. So too is the famous flame lily, *Gloriosa superba*. This handsome bulbous scrambler occurs naturally in the eastern parts of the country and thence up into central Africa. It is found in a range of colour forms, yellow and orange being the most common.

1. *Aloe microstigma*

2. *Daubenya aurea*

Liliaceae usually have symmetrical or nearly symmetrical flowers, but in *Daubenya*, a unique monotypic genus from the Roggeveld, Northern Cape Province, the outermost flowers in each flowerhead are strongly asymmetrical.

From the simple basic flower structure of this family many variations have been developed. *Androcymbium* has dull insignificant flowers made conspicuous by prominent white bracts (modified leaves) that subtend the flowerhead. A different strategy is adopted by *Sandersonia aurantiaca*, the scarce Christmas bells of the KwaZulu-Natal Midlands, in which the six coloured petals which make up each flower are not free but fused to form a lantern-like bloom.

3. *Aloe ferox:* Bitteraalwyn, Tapaalwyn, Goreebosch

4. *Bulbinella nutans* var. *turfosicola*

5. *Aloe broomii:* Slangaalwyn, Bergaalwee

. *Lachenalia sargeantii*

7. *Pseudogaltonia clavata:* Gifbol, Groenlelie

8. *Kniphofia praecox:* Red-hot poker

9. *Lachenalia aloides* var. *aurea:* Geelklipkalossie, Geelviooltjie

10. *Androcymbium striatum:* Bobbejaanskoen, Patrysblom

11. *Agapanthus inapertus*

12. *Sandersonia aurantiaca:* Christmas bells, Geelklokkie

13. *Gloriosa superba:* Flame lily

4. *Ornithogalum dubium:* Geeltjienkerintjee

5. *Gloriosa superba:* Flame lily

16. *Agapanthus africanus:* Agapanthus, Bloulelie

AMARYLLIDACEAE

This family occurs all over the world and is comparatively well developed in South Africa, where at least 250 species are found.

Brunsvigia, a genus found mainly in the Western and Northern Cape provinces, clearly demonstrates the umbellate flowerhead in which each flower branches from the same point on the stalk. In autumn, a stout flower-spike emerges from a football-sized bulb, pushes through hard earth, and then unfurls to form a brilliant globe. When it fades, the main stalk separates from the bulb at ground level and tumbles along the ground, scattering seed. Leaves appear later with the first winter rains.

Scadoxus puniceus is a subtropical species from the Eastern Cape Province, KwaZulu-Natal and Mpumalanga. *Ammocharis coranica*, frequent in the summer rainfall area, often forms massed displays. In Lesotho, a gluey paste made from cooked *Ammocharis* bulbs is used to mend cracks in clay pots.

There are only four species of *Clivia*, all of them endemic to South Africa. *C. miniata* from the forests of KwaZulu-Natal has been a garden favourite for over a century. The common orange form is shown here, but the rare clear yellow is also sometimes seen.

Crinums are among the most robust South African amaryllids, occasionally producing flower-spikes over a metre high. More modest is *Crinum campanulatum*, an unusual aquatic species often seen growing partly submerged in Eastern Cape vleis.

18. *Brunsvigia orientalis:* Candelabra flower; Koningskandelaarblom

19. *Brunsvigia marginata*

17. *Scadoxus puniceus:* Paintbrush, Poeierkwas

20. *Ammocharis coranica:* Gifbol, Seeroogblom

21. *Clivia miniata:* Bush lily, Boslelie

22. *Crinum campanulatum:* Vleilelie

23. *Cyrtanthus breviflorus*

Cyrtanthus is another large genus. Several species are popularly called fire lilies because of their habit of bursting into flower after a veld fire. This is especially true of the Western Cape species, *C. ventricosus*, frequently seen a fortnight after the veld has been destroyed by fire, illuminating an ashen landscape.

In its natural state, *Amaryllis belladonna*, the March lily, responds similarly to fire, but tends to bloom more regularly when cultivated.

Kukumakranka is the popular name for *Gethyllis*, of which there are a dozen species in the Western Cape Province and the Namaqualand region. The delicately perfumed flowers are followed in late autumn by deliciously aromatic cylindrical fruits, used by farmers to flavour liqueur brandy.

Many other amaryllids have fleshy fruits, especially obvious in *Haemanthus*, where the flowers precede shiny crimson berries.

Boophane disticha, the 'gifbol', is used by indigenous people of South Africa to poison their arrows. Like *Brunsvigia*, its spent heads tumble about in the wind dispersing their seeds.

Nerine, a genus of some 30 species, is one of South Africa's greatest contributions to the world's gardens. Most hybrids have the Western Cape *N. sarniensis* in their parentage.

25. *Cyrtanthus ventricosus:* Brandlelie

24. *Cyrtanthus contractus:* Fire lily, Vuurlelie

6. *Amaryllis belladonna:* Belladonna lily, Belladonnalelie

27. *Gethyllis britteniana:* Kukumakranka, Koekoemakranka

8. *Clivia nobilis:* Bush lily, Boslelie

29. *Haemanthus sanguineus:* April-fool, Velskoenblaar

30. *Haemanthus sanguineus*

31. *Brunsvigia gregaria*

32. *Cyrtanthus sanguineus:* Ifafa lily, Keilelie

33. *Cybistetes longifolia:* Malagash lily, Malgaslelie

34. *Apodolirion ettae*

35. *Boophane disticha:* Poison bulb, Seeroogblom

36. *Boophane disticha:* Poison bulb, Seeroogblom

37. *Nerine sarniensis:* Guernsey lily, Berglelie

HAEMODORACEAE

38. *Wachendorfia thyrsiflora:* Rooikanol

The root systems of plants seldom possess characters which can be used as an aid to identification at family level. However, in the Haemodoraceae or blood-root family, both the rhizomatous and cormous rootstocks, at least in the South African species, all contain brilliant orange-red pigments. This small family is best developed in countries of the Southern Hemisphere and is represented in South Africa by about 15 species. *Dilatris* and *Wachendorfia* are the largest genera.

Wachendorfia thyrsiflora, a spectacular streamside plant from the Western Cape mountains, has prominently pleated leaves and produces two-metre-tall yellow flower-spikes in springtime. *Dilatris corymbosa* tends to appear in drier mountain areas of the Western Cape Province, while *D. viscosa* is only found in permanently moist areas on the higher peaks.

39. *Dilatris corymbosa:* Rooiwortel

40. *Wachendorfia thyrsiflora:* Rooikanol

41. *Dilatris viscosa*

APONOGETONACEAE

This exclusively aquatic family consists of a single genus, *Aponogeton*, which is found mainly in Africa, Madagascar and Australia. Of the 25 species, seven occur in South Africa, the best-known species being *A. distachyos*, the 'waterblommetjie' or 'wateruintjie'. White, bilobed, sweetly scented flowerheads appear in late winter and spring, floating among the leaves on Cape vleis, or other shallow expanses of water. The mature flowerheads are the major ingredient in a highly esteemed traditional dish, waterblommetjiebredie (a stew of mutton and waterblommetjies). Demand is so great that the blooms are now canned commercially and some farmers are even cultivating them in artificial ponds.

As natural vleis dry up in summer the plants die back to resting subterranean rhizomes until the winter rains begin, when they sprout again to start a new growth cycle.

A. distachyos, being an interesting aquatic, has long been cultivated abroad as the Cape water hawthorn.

42. *Aponogeton distachyos:* Cape pondweed, Waterblommetjie

VELLOZIACEAE

In South Africa this small tropical to subtropical family comprises only two genera, *Xerophyta* and *Talbotia*. *Xerophyta* is the largest and most conspicuous genus with about six species found in the Northern Province, Mpumalanga, Swaziland and KwaZulu-Natal. Several, like *Xerophyta viscosa*, are tall-stemmed. The strange growth habit of these plants at once attracts attention: they appear as blackened stumps covered by hard fibrous layers with tufts of coarse, grass-like leaves at the tip of each stem. In spring these apparently dead stumps come to life as delicate mauve blooms appear from their tips. Xerophytas are generally found in and around rocky habitats. These plants survive frequent burning and may grow to anything from a metre to three metres in height. They are usually called 'bobbejaanstert' or black-stick lilies.

43. *Xerophyta viscosa*

44. *Xerophyta viscosa*

HYPOXIDACEAE

Some botanists classify members of this family among the Amaryllidaceae but, especially in South Africa, they form a very distinct group. The family is largely confined to the Southern Hemisphere and comprises approximately 130 species in eight genera. Over half that number of species, grouped in six genera is found in South Africa which clearly suggests that the Hypoxidaceae has undergone considerable evolutionary diversification in this region. All our hypoxids are geophytes, that is, they survive the dry season with corms of rhizomatous rootstocks. *Hypoxis* itself is a rather nondescript genus of yellow-flowered herbaceous species found mainly in Gauteng, Mpumalanga and KwaZulu-Natal grassveld.

But *Spiloxene* is the most beguiling genus of some 30 species dispersed throughout the Western Cape Province where they are commonly called 'sterretjies': the two peacock-eyed *Spiloxenes*, *Spiloxene capensis* and *Spiloxene canaliculata*, are the ones most admired. They appear in damp fields or along ditches and seepage areas, flowering in spring and often growing together. *S. capensis* may be plain yellow or white, or white or pink with a peacock-eye at the centre. The eye is formed from patches of black, purple or iridescent green at the base of each petal. *S. canaliculata* also has an eye, but it is usually orange or yellow.

Equally charming but seldom seen is *Rhodohypoxis baurii*, one of the gems of the high Drakensberg. Its tolerance of severe frost has made this exquisite miniature a favourite with alpine gardeners in Britain. The petal colour covers a wide range, from pure white to deep burgundy, but is most commonly a shade of pink.

45. *Spiloxene curculigoides:* Sterretjie

47. *Spiloxene capensis:* Golden star, Geelsterretjie

46. *Spiloxene canaliculata:* Geelsterretjie

48. *Rhodohypoxis baurii:* Rooisterretjie

49. *Spiloxene capenis:* Golden star, Geelsterretjie

50. *Rhodohypoxis baurii:* Rooisterretjie

IRIDACEAE

51. *Romulea monticola:* Frutang, Froetang

52. *Babiana rubrocyanea:* Kelkiewyn

The iris family is cosmopolitan in its distribution and comprises some 1 660 species, but in South Africa it is probably better developed than elsewhere. Over 900 species are found here – more than half the world total for the family. By far the greatest majority occur in the Western Cape Province and Namaqualand. *Gladiolus*, with about 135 species, is our largest genus.

Over the past two centuries many South African irids have been domesticated and are now familiar garden plants, such as gladioli, freesias, crocosmias, ixias and watsonias. Some of the irids have been so 'improved' by plant breeders that often it is not easy to associate modern garden hybrids with their humble wild ancestors in the veld.

Most of the Cape genera are deciduous, sprouting from underground corms with the advent of the wet season, flowering, and then dying back and becoming dormant during the dry season. *Moraea, Hesperantha, Romulea, Geissorhiza, Gladiolus* and *Babiana* are among the larger genera which are common in the Western Cape Province, flowering in autumn, winter and spring.

Watsonia is one of the more robust and is dispersed throughout the country. Several species are evergreen and most tend to flower profusely after veld fires. In fact, certain watsonias such as *W. zeyheri* will only flower after burning and actually need a veld fire to initiate the flowering process.

Nivenia and *Witsenia* are unique in that they have a shrubby growth habit with woody stems, lacking any underground corms or rhizomes. Both are found only in the mountains of the Western Cape Province.

In KwaZulu-Natal and Mpumalanga, clumps of *Dierama*, sometimes called hairbells, are seen in moist grassveld, while at higher elevations in these areas pink or red *Schizostylis* brighten the margins of mountain streams. Both are frequently cultivated, as are the handsome *Dietes* from the Eastern Cape Province and KwaZulu-Natal. Flowers in the Iridaceae family come in every known colour and colour combination. Some are almost transparent, such as

53. *Hesperantha vaginata*

54. *Babiana villosa:* Rooibobbejaantjie

55. *Nivenia stokoei*

56. *Moraea tricolor*

57. *Watsonia zeyheri*

58. *Watsonia tabularis*

59. *Schizostylis coccinea:* Kaffir lily, Kafferlelie

60. *Aristea spiralis*

61. *Dierama galpinii*

62. *Geissorhiza ovata*

63. *Gladiolus bonaespei:*
lames, Rooi-afrikaner

64. *Dietes grandiflora*

65. *Crocosmia aurea*

66. *Ixia viridiflora:* Green ixia, Groenkalossie

67. *Gladiolus cardinalis:*
Waterfall gladiolus, Nuwejaarsafrikaner

68. *Gladiolus maculatus:* Aandblom

Gladiolus hyalinus, but the most astonishing is the turquoise green *Ixia viridiflora* which is found in Tulbagh in the Western Cape Province. Other genera, for example, *Hesperantha,* open towards evening while certain moraeas and aristeas have such delicate ephemeral petals that after opening for a few hours they simply wither away.

Iridaceae are of little economic value but are of considerable horticultural importance. *Moraea polystachya* and several species of *Homeria* are poisonous to both man and beast, but the majority of other genera have edible corms. These were consumed by primitive man, and even today in remote country districts, especially Namaqualand, irid corms, or 'uintjies', are gathered by locals and eaten, raw or roasted.

69. *Romulea eximia:* Frutang, Froetang

70. *Gladiolus hyalinus:* Kliplelie, Klippypie

71. *Gladiolus maculatus:* Aandblom

72. *Gladiolus alatus:* Kalkoentjie

73. *Anapalina caffra*

74. *Witsenia maura:* Bokmakieriestert

POACEAE

Grasses, so rarely illustrated in books on wild flowers, belong to a huge cosmopolitan family, the Poaceae (also known as Gramineae). Approximately 9 000 species are dispersed over the globe from the fringes of the polar wastes to the equator. Although it can be said that they are the most important plants on earth, for they provide man with such essentials as cereals, sugar and grazing for his stock, these ubiquitous plants are easily overlooked. In South Africa about 750 species have been recorded, forming much of the plant cover in summer rainfall areas. *Melinis repens*, red-top grass, is perhaps the most beautiful of our grasses. Originally from KwaZulu-Natal and Mpumalanga, it is now naturalized in parts of the Western Cape Province.

75. *Melinis repens:* Natal red-top, Bergrooigras

77. *Hyphaene natalensis:* Ilala palm

78. *Raphia australis:* Raphia palm

ARECACEAE (PALMAE)

Palms are essentially tropical or subtropical trees and belong to a large par tropical family. Only five species are indigenous to South Africa and all grow i the warmer parts of the country. The most unusual is the mkambati palm *Jubaeopsis caffra*, only found at three localities along the Eastern Cape coas *Hyphaene ventricosa* is perhaps the most typical of our palms, often seen in th Kruger National Park. *Raphia australis* from the KwaZulu-Natal coast is a mono carpic (fruiting once only) species taking years to grow to maturity: and then flowers once and dies.

The Raphia palm's strong leaf midribs are used by black people for buildir huts as well as their traditional rafts that are still used on the Kosi lake system c northern KwaZulu-Natal.

76. *Jubaeopsis caffra:*
Pondoland coconut, Palmboom

STRELITZIACEAE

Only five different species represent this small pan-tropical family in South Africa, but all are handsome plants, producing most arresting flowers and leaves.

Strelitzia reginae, the crane flower, is herbaceous. It grows up to two metres high in its natural habitat, the Eastern Cape coastal bush, and it is cultivated by commercial growers in most warm countries for its magnificent orange, blue and white blooms: pale yellow mutants are occasionally seen. The white and blue flowered species are trees up to ten metres high with enormous stalked leaves. *S. alba* (Knysna to Humansdorp) and *S. nicolai* (East London to KwaZulu-Natal) are found in coastal areas, to which they give a distinctly exotic tropical atmosphere, while *S. caudata*, similar in appearance, grows only in the Northern Province.

79. *Strelitzia nicolai:* Natal strelitzia

80. *Strelitzia nicolai:* Natal strelitzia

81. *Strelitzia reginae:* Bird of Paradise flower, Wildepiesang

ARACEAE

Most aroids grow in the tropics or subtropics, but a number do occur in temperate regions where they usually become deciduous and are either bulbous or rhizomatous.

Zantedeschia is an exclusively South African genus of six species, popularly known as arum lilies. Each 'flower' is in fact a composite structure consisting of a coloured spathe or sheathing bract enclosing a finger-like spadix, a fleshy spine bearing hundreds of minute, individual flowers. *Z. aethiopica*, the commonest species, is white and has become almost a weed in its native Western Cape Province, adorning ditches, vleis and streamsides from early winter to late spring. Forms of this species with greenish spathes are occasionally seen. In Mpumalanga grow the yellow-flowered *Z. pentlandii*, the tiny pink-flowered *Z. rehmannii* and the cream-coloured *Z. albomaculata* with its spotted leaves.

82. *Zantedeschia aethiopica* (form): Arum lily, Varklelie

83. *Zantedeschia aethiopica:* Arum lily, Varklelie

4. *Zantedeschia pentlandii*

85. *Zantedeschia albomaculata:* Kleinvarkblom

86. *Zantedeschia pentlandii*

87. *Zantedeschia rehmannii:* Purple arum, Persvarkblom

88. *Zantedeschia rehmannii:* Purple arum, Persvarkblom

ORCHIDACEAE

Orchids form one of the largest families of plants in the world, some 18 000 species in all, of which about 550 grow wild in South Africa. They are highly prized for their spectacular flowers, especially those of tropical epiphytic species (that is, growing on another plant but not parasitic).

Ansellia africana is the largest of our epiphytic orchids. It is occasionally seen flowering in the crowns of bushveld trees in the Lowveld and in KwaZulu-Natal.

However, most South African orchids are terrestrial or ground-dwelling species such as *Disa* (70 species) and *Satyrium* (40 species), our largest genera. The famous red disa, *D. uniflora*, which grows beside streams and waterfalls in the Western Cape mountains, is probably the most magnificent red-flowered orchid known. *Disperis, Herschelianthe* and *Ceratandra* are genera from the high Cape mountains. Like many other bulbous or tuberous plants in the Cape, they tend to be stimulated to flower by burning, often flowering profusely after a veld fire only to 'disappear' until the next one stimulates them to bloom again.

Bartholina burmanniana, a tiny, delicate species with a deeply incised lower lip, is commonly called the spider orchid. It tends to grow concealed under bushes, where it is easily overlooked, but is found on heavy clay soils in many parts of the Western Cape Province, flowering in spring.

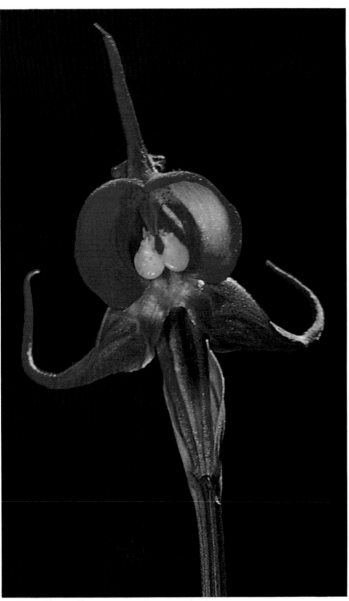

89. *Disperis capensis:* Granny-bonnet, Moederkappie

90. *Herschelianthe graminifolia:* Blue Disa, Bloumoederkappie

91. *Bartholina burmanniana:* Spider orchid, Spinnekopblom

92. *Disa grandulosa*

93. *Disa uniflora:* Pride of Table Mountain, Rooidisa

94. *Ceratandra grandiflora*

95. *Disa filicornis*

6. *Disa atricapilla*

97. *Satyrium coriifolia:* Ewwa-trewwa

98. *Ansellia africana:* Tiger orchid

MORACEAE

This is the family to which figs and mulberries belong. *Ficus* – the figs – is the largest genus, containing over 1 000 species distributed over most of the warmer regions of the world. In South Africa there are about 25 species of *Ficus* all producing edible though rather dry, insipid fruits. The fig fruit itself is actually a collection of hundreds of tiny flowers arranged inside a globe-like structure with a distinct pore or opening at one end. When fully developed the pore opens to admit tiny, highly specialized flies which crawl inside and pollinate the individual flowers. Apart from their characteristic fruits (figs), all *Ficus* species exude a white milky latex when a stem or leaf stalk is snapped. *Ficus sur*, the Cape fig, is our most widespread species, ranging from the Southern Cape to the Northern Province and Mpumalanga; it is also probably our most beautiful, producing long, pendulous trusses of bright pink figs from its main branches. Most figs are exceptionally handsome trees, especially *F. sansibaric* which can be seen in many parts of the Lowveld. This species may become a strangler, starting life as a seedling in a branch cleft on a host tree, eventually putting out aerial roots, and ultimately enveloping and later strangling the host species on which it originally germinated. *Ficus glumosa* is also equipped with powerful roots but is a rock-splitter rather than a strangler. Here a seed sometimes germinates in a rock crevice, forcing the rocks asunder as the roots grow and mature, snaking their way between exposed fissure lines.

99. *Ficus sur:* Cape fig

100. *Ficus glumosa:* Mountain rock fig

101. *Ficus sansibarica:* Zanzibar fig

PROTEACEAE

South Africa and Australia are the two most important centres of distribution for this characteristically Southern Hemisphere family. About 450 species are found in South Africa where *Protea* (83 species), *Leucadendron* (82 species) and *Leucospermum* (49 species) are the largest genera. Most of the family is concentrated in the South Western Cape Province where proteaceous plants make up an important broad-leaved shrubby component of fynbos vegetation. *Protea cynaroides*, a widely-dispersed species from mountainous country between Citrusdal and Grahamstown is South Africa's national flower with flowerheads up to 30 cm in diameter. Proteas are named after

102. *Mimetes cucullatus:* Rooistompie

the Greek god Proteus, who had the ability to change his shape and take on many forms. Some are trees (*P. nitida*), or shrubs (*P. neriifolia*) while others have a low tufted growth habit as in *P. cryophila*, the snow protea from the high Cedarberg Mountains. Most brightly coloured shrubby species are pollinated by the Cape sugarbird, seen here on *P. cynaroides*. Sugarbirds feed both on nectar and tiny insects in the flowerheads.

103. *Mimetes hirtus*

104. *Protea cynaroides:* Giant protea

105. *Leucospermum glabrum:* George pincushion

106. *Leucospermum reflexum*

107. *Protea compacta*

108. *Protea cynaroides:* Giant protea

09. *Protea nitida*

110. *Protea stokoei:* Stokoe's protea

111. *Protea neriifolia:* Blousuikerbos

112. *Protea lorifolia*

113. *Leucospermum cordifolium:* Pincushion

14. *Protea aurea*

115. *Leucadendron tinctum* (female)

116. *Mimetes hottentoticus:* Matchstick mimetes

117. *Protea obtusifolia:* Bredasdorp protea

118. *Leucadendron salignum:* Tolbos

119. *Serruria florida:* Blushing bride

120. *Leucospermum tottum*

Several different natural evolutionary strategies have been adopted over the years to produce a variety of brilliant flowerheads in this family. Brightly coloured leaves, also known as bracts, surround each flowerhead in *Protea*, but in *Leucospermum* (pincushions) and *Mimetes* it is the colourful styles that create a spectacular show. *Leucadendron* (also known as geelbos) has male and female flowers on different plants; the female flower differs from the male flower by being massed in woody cones. *Paranomus* and *Serruria* rely on both styles and perianths to produce their unique display. *Serruria florida*, also known as the blushing bride, is a rare species in its natural habitat at Assegaaibos in the Franschhoek Mountains in the Western Cape Province, but its horticultural popularity has happily ensured its security as a species.

121. *Protea cryophila:* Snow protea

122. *Leucadendron laureolum:* Geelbos

123. *Leucadendron conicum*

124. *Leucadendron linifolium*

125. *Serruria cyanoides*

126. *Leucospermum calligerum*

127. *Leucospermum truncatum*

128. *Leucadendron spissifolium:* Vleitolbos

MESEMBRYANTHEMACEAE

Vygies (little figs), is a popular name for many members of the great pan-tropical family which is centred in South Africa where over 2 000 species are found and where climate variations have caused the Mesembryanthemaceae numerous diversities as they adapted to conditions of great aridity and in so doing evolving some bizarre growth forms. The greatest species concentrations are found in Namaqualand and the Little Karoo. Mesembryanthemum means 'midday flower' and denotes its habit of opening towards midday in warm sunny weather, and closing on dull days and at night. All are succulents but the degree of fleshiness varies from genus to genus. *Lampranthus* are generally shrubby: *L. roseus* in pink, white and red colour forms and the yellow *L. aureus* are two of our most widely cultivated vygies. At the other extreme are dwarf genera such as *Conophytum, Pleiospilos* and *Lithops*, which have one or more spherical 'bodies', each composed of a pair of fused leaves. Sometimes an adult plant is reduced to a single pair of leaves as in *Lithops*, the stone plants. Mimicry is an important feature of these genera, particularly in *Conophytum* whose speckled bodies often resemble the lichenous encrustations on rocks in whose cracks and crevices it is to be found, while *Lithops* matches the colour and even the texture of the stones and rocks amongst which it grows so successfully that it often escapes detection by hungry animals.

Fenestraria – the name means a collection of windows – is even more remarkable. Here whole plants are buried in loose sand which protects them from blistering heat and intense sunlight. Only the tops of the cylindrical leaves emerge above the sand, their tips being provided with lens-like 'windows' admitting just sufficient light to sustain photosynthesis. These astonishing 'window-plants' can be found in the southern parts of the Namib Desert and at the Orange River mouth.

129. *Lampranthus roseus:* Red vygie

30. *Lampranthus aureus:* Golden vygie

131. *Fenestraria rhopalophylla*

32. *Lampranthus watermeyeri*

133. *Pleiospilos nelii:* Kwaggavygie

34. *Conophytum pellucidum*

135. *Lithops ruschiorum:* Stone plant

137. *Drosanthemum speciosum*

136. *Carpobrotus quadrifidus*

138. *Dorotheanthus rourkei*

139. *Dorotheanthus bellidiformis:* Bokbaaivygie

Conicosia and *Carpobrotus* are trailing perennials. In *Carpobrotus*, soft edible fruits containing an acid pulp appear a few weeks after the dazzling flowers have faded. These are gathered and sold as 'sour figs'. *Dorotheanthus* is a genus of succulent annuals; *D. bellidiformis*, the famous Bokbaaivygie, grows wild along the West Coast between Milnerton and Saldanha, and is a great spring favourite in gardens the world over; *D. rourkei*, a rare Namaqualand species, has hitherto defied attempts to cultivate it.

40. *Conicosia pugioniformis:* Varkslaai

LORANTHACEAE

About 50 species of this essentially tropical to subtropical family – popularly called mistletoes – are found in South Africa. All are parasites, growing on other trees or shrubs: but only partial parasites, drawing water and nutrients from their hosts but producing carbohydrates from their own green stems and leaves. *Viscum* (true mistletoe) accounts for about half the local species while the remainder are placed in various other genera.

Loranthus and *Tapinanthus* are especially colourful when in bloom, so much so that many an apparently floriferous tree on closer inspection often turns out to be heavily infested with *Loranthus* or *Tapinanthus* in full bloom! *Tapinanthus rubromarginatus* is common in Mpumalanga, usually on *Acacia* trees.

The flowers are followed by sticky, edible berries on which birds feed and which stick to their beaks and are then wiped off on the branches of another host, where the seeds soon germinate, putting out a strong root which bores into the vascular tissue of the host tree, thus starting a new life-cycle.

141. *Tapinanthus rubromarginatus*

AMARANTHACEAE

This rather unprepossessing, pan-tropical family has the dubious distinction of counting many troublesome agricultural weeds among its ranks. However, a few garden plants, for example *Celosia* (cockscomb), also belong here. It is rather well represented in South Africa, especially in the arid western and central regions of the country where annual and herbaceous species flourish on the meagre rainfall of occasional summer thundershowers. *Hermbstaedtia odorata* shows the family's typical feature, namely, tiny massed flowerheads with each flower surrounded by dry, chaffy coloured tracts.

142. *Hermbstaedtia odorata:* Katstert

RANUNCULACEAE

Although centred mainly in cool temperate parts of the Northern Hemisphere, the Ranunculus family does have about 25 species indigenous to South Africa, mainly in the genus *Knowltonia*. A rhizomatous perennial, common in coastal bush and forested kloofs, *Knowltonia capensis* is a very handsome green-flowered species.

Anemone tenuifolia is an evergreen perennial from the higher Cape mountains. It flowers rather erratically under normal conditions but blooms profusely after veld fires making a splendid show in white, pink or cerise. Traveller's joy is the common name for *Clematis brachiata*, a rampant, sweetly scented climber which festoons both bush and forest margins in the Eastern Cape Province, Northern Province, Mpumalanga and KwaZulu-Natal during December and January.

144. *Knowltonia capensis:* Katjieblaar

143. *Clematis brachiata:* Traveller's joy, Klimop

145. *Anemone tenuifolia:* Anemone, Syblom

NYMPHAEACEAE

Nymphaea is the principal genus of this small but distinctive family, popularly called water lilies. It is cosmopolitan and represented in South Africa by two species of which the most widespread is the mauve-blue Cape water lily, *N. nouchali* var. *caerulea.*

This species formerly occurred in vleis on the Cape Peninsula but is now extinct there, although it still survives in dams, vleis and in quiet backwaters of major rivers in many other parts of the country.

The other indigenous water lily *Nymphaea lotus* with creamy white flowers is seen only occasionally in Kwazulu-Natal and the warmer parts of Mpumalanga.

146. *Nymphaea nouchali* var. *caerulea:* Water lily, Paddapreekstoel

DROSERACEAE

147. *Drosera cistiflora:* Sundew, Doublom

150. *Drosera hilaris*

151. *Drosera trinervia*

148. *Drosera cistiflora:* Sundew, Doublom

These captivating, insectivorous plants, called sundews, all belong to the genus *Drosera* of which there are 18 species in South Africa. They are easily recognized by their leaves which are covered with sticky, sensitive, stalked glands. Flies and other small insects are trapped in these glands and are absorbed to augment the plants' nitrogen supply.

Drosera cistiflora, a large-flowered Western Cape species, is usually pink, white or cream but a brilliant scarlet colour form is found at a few sites near Darling, north of Cape Town. *D. cistiflora* and the diminutive *D. trinervia* are both tuberous, dying down and becoming dormant in summer and then sprouting and growing again with the advent of winter rains, while *D. hilaris* is an ever-green herbaceous species.

149. *Drosera cistiflora:* Sundew, Doublom

152. *Drosera cistiflora:* Sundew, Doublom

BRASSICACEAE (CRUCIFERAE)

The cabbage family has several representatives in South Africa but *Heliophila*, a genus of some 70 species, is the most important. Most heliophilas are delicate winter-growing annuals flowering in August and September. The majority have vivid blue flowers and are popularly called blue flax although several white and yellow flow-ered species are known. From the Darling-Malmesbury area of the Western Cape to Northern Namaqualand one can be sure that any large patch of intensely blue flowers seen in the veld during spring-time is one or other of the heliophilas in bloom. They tend mainly to open on warm sunny days – the name *Heliophila* means sun-lover.

53. *Heliophila coronopifolia*

154. *Heliophila africana*

OCHNACEAE

Ochna and *Brackenridgea* are the only South African genera of this largely South American-centred family of tropical and sub-tropical trees and shrubs.

Ochna's have become much-loved garden shrubs especially *O. ser-rulata* and *O. natalitia*. Spectacular as their golden trusses of flowers may be in springtime, it is their gaudy fruits which catch the eye and indeed have inspired their common name, Mickey Mouse tree. After flowering the calyx-lobes turn red, reflexing to reveal the at first green and then later shiny black seeds. At this stage the whole structure looks uncommonly like a Mickey Mouse face!

Ochna is found from the Eastern Cape Province and KwaZulu-Natal to Mpumalanga and the Northern Province.

55. *Ochna serrulata:*
Mickey Mouse tree, Carnival bush, Rooihout

156. *Ochna natalitia:* Rooihout

157 *Ochna pulchra:* Wild pear, Wildepruim

CRASSULACEAE

Like several other predominantly succulent plant families, the cosmopolitan Crassulaceae is centred in South Africa where it has undergone great diversification, and adapted to a variety of habitats. Practically all are succulents: indeed, the family name is derived from the Latin, *crassus*, meaning thick.

Crassula, the largest genus in this family, is represented here by over 140 species. In the Karoo and Namaqualand crassulas are plump, dwarf succulents with tightly overlapping leaves as in *C. pyramidalis* and *C. columnaris*. Others, like the scarlet *C. coccinea*, grow in the mistbelt region of the high Cape peaks, while *C. fascicularis* is a herbaceous, fynbos species and *C. vaginata* is frequent in grassland habitats in Mpumalanga and KwaZulu-Natal. *Crassula ovata* from the Eastern Cape bush grows into a small tree up to three metres in height.

Cotyledon, a related genus, contains several species highly toxic to stock but the fleshy leaves of the variable and wide-spread *Cotyledon orbiculata* have long been successfully used by many people to soften and remove corns and warts.

158. *Crassula pyramidalis:* Rygbossie

159. *Crassula coccinea:* Red crassula, Klipblom

160. *Crassula fascicularis:* Klipblom 161. *Crassula coccinea:* Red crassula, Klipblom 162. *Crassula vaginata*

164. *Crassula fascicularis:* Klipblom

165. *Crassula corallina*

163. *Crassula columnaris* 166. *Crassula fascicularis:* Klipblom

167. *Cotyledon orbiculata:* Pig's ears, Varkore

168. *Crassula vaginata*

169. *Crassula ovata:* Karkay, Plakkies

170. *Crassula perfoliata:* Red crassula, Heuningbossie

CUNONIACEAE

71. *Cunonia capensis:* Red alder, Rooi-els

Only two members of this small Southern Hemisphere family are found in South Africa – *Platylophus trifoliatus* and *Cunonia capensis*, better known as 'rooi-els'.

Cunonia capensis is a handsome forest tree, frequent in moist evergreen forests from the Cape to as far north as Mpumalanga, often attaining 18 metres in height. Apart from producing beautiful timber, rooi-els is one of our most decorative trees. Creamy white flower spikes, like candles, appear among the dark glossy foliage in May and June, greatly enlivening the sombre forests at a time when few other trees are flowering.

C. capensis is an isolated outlier: all other species of *Cunonia* are confined to the Pacific island of New Caledonia.

ROSACEAE

72. *Grielum humifusum*: Duikerwortel

The Rose family is a huge cosmopolitan assemblage of plants, many of them of great economic importance, but in South Africa represented by only about 120 species, mostly spiny, rather insignificant shrubs. *Grielum*, a genus of about five eye-catching species, is the only exception. These trailing annuals or perennials grow in winter, mainly in the more arid region of the Western Cape Province and Namaqualand. On warm, sunny springtime days their brilliant yellow, satin-textured flowers burst open, carpeting the veld with a dazzling but ephemeral display. Not surprisingly, many attempts have been made to cultivate these gorgeous plants away from their natural habitats, but hitherto without success. Even at Kirstenbosch where grielums have on occasion been grown, the flowers often fail to open properly due to insufficient light intensity.

BRUNIACEAE

This small but distinctive family of approximately eighty species occurs only in South Africa, and even here it is restricted to the Western Cape Province, growing almost exclusively on Table Mountain sandstone formations. They are heath-like shrubs with tiny flowers often massed in spherical heads. *Audouinia capitata*, a species confined to the Cape Peninsula, is heath-like in appearance while *Staavia* has

173. *Brunia stokoei:* Rooistompie

compound flowerheads resembling those of the daisy family. *Brunia*, *Berzelia* and *Nebelia* are the largest and most typical genera with their massed pompon-shaped flowerheads.

Berzelia lanuginosa, illustrated here, is one of the most widespread species. This plant grows in dense stands particularly along watercourses or in seepage areas where its presence is regarded as a sure indicator of perennial water.

174. *Staavia glutinosa:*
Flycatcher bush, Vlieëbossie

175. *Brunia nodiflora:*
Stompie, Fonteinbossie

176. *Berzelia lanuginosa:* Kol-kol

177. *Audouinia capitata:* False heath, Basterheide

178. *Berzelia lanuginosa:* Vleiknopbos, Kol-kol

179. *Nebelia paleacea*

FABACEAE (LEGUMINOSAE)

180. *Aspalathus carnosa*

Leguminous plants (pod and bean bearers) constitute one of the largest and most economically important plant families in the world. Some botanists prefer to subdivide them into three separate families but it is more convenient to regard them as a single family, Fabaceae (or Leguminosae as it is alternatively called).

South Africa is well endowed with legumes to be found in every part of the country, many of them beautiful trees or shrubs. *Priestleya*, *Podalyria*, *Liparia* and *Hypocalyptus* are all from the fynbos area of the South Western Cape Province while *Adenolobus* is characteristic of the arid Northern Cape Province.

Soft-wooded herbaceous forms of this family such as the widely dispersed *Sutherlandia frutescens* are also common. *Sutherlandia* is cultivated for both its flowers and its ornamental inflated pods, but is best known by most people for its supposed medicinal properties.

Commonly called 'kankerbossie' in country districts it is believed that an infusion of the leaves cures cancer.

Thorn trees, belonging to the genus *Acacia*, are also legumes. They are the most ubiquitous and typical of our native trees. There are over 40 species indigenous to South Africa, found throughout the country but especially in KwaZulu-Natal, the Northern Province and Mpumalanga.

Their tiny yellow or cream flowers are massed in spherical clusters or slender cylindrical spikes. *Dichrostachys cinerea*, a common Bushveld tree, looks very like an *Acacia* but is easily distinguished by its bicoloured flower-spikes in pink and yellow.

In warmer parts of the Eastern Cape Province and KwaZulu-Natal one is likely to encounter one or other of the more than eight native species of *Erythrina*, or coral trees, surely the most spectacular of all

181. *Bauhinia galpinii*: Pride of De Kaap, Vlam-van-die-Vlakte

182. *Acacia ataxacantha*: Flame thorn, Vlamdoring

183. *Sutherlandia frutescens:* Cancer bush

84. *Crotalaria doidgeae*

185. *Priestleya tomentosa:* Silver pea, Vaalertjie

186. *Schotia afra:* Small-leaved Karoo Boer-bean, Fynblaarkarooboerboon

187. *Erythrina latissima:* Broad-leaved coral tree

188. *Adenolobus pechuelii*

our ornamental trees. Several species have the habit of producing trusses of scarlet blooms in late spring, just before the summer flush of new leaves has appeared.

Many legumes have nitrogen-fixing bacteria in nodules on their roots and so while we frequently tend to evaluate these plants in aesthetic terms it should be remembered that they also play a key role in improving the nitrogen levels in the soil.

189. *Liparia splendens:*
Orange nodding-head,
Mountain dahlia, Geelkoppie

190. *Erythrina humeana:* Dwarf coral tree, Kleinkoraalboom

91. *Dichrostachys cinerea:* Sickle bush, Sekelbos

192. *Bolusanthus speciosus:* Tree wisteria, Vanwykshout

Bolusanthus speciosus, although small in stature, is one of our most graceful trees. It is found in the Mpumalanga bushveld, producing pendulous sprays of mauve flowers in spring. They closely resemble *Wisteria* but are without any scent. The generic name *Bolusanthus* means 'Bolus flower' and honours Dr Harry Bolus, the pioneer Cape botanist who founded the Bolus Herbarium.

194. *Hypocalyptus sophoroides*

93. *Acacia nebrownii:* Water thorn, Waterdoring

OXALIDACEAE

Most of the more than 200 South African species of *Oxalis* are found in Namaqualand and the Western Cape Province, but a few such as *O. smithiana* reach KwaZulu-Natal and Mpumalanga. At the Cape they are the harbingers of winter, appearing almost everywhere and flowering from autumn throughout winter into spring. Their deep-seated bulbs are so sensitive to the change of season that even before the first autumn rains have fallen, early flowering species break through the parched earth and burst into bloom. They come in almost every colour except blue, either as single flowers as in *O. purpurea* or massed together like a Victorian posy as in *O. heidelbergensis*. Commonly called sorrel or 'surings' because of the tart acidic flavour of the leaves and stems, several species with fairly large, edible, nutty-flavoured bulbs are sometimes collected and eaten in the Northern Cape: but this old practice is fast disappearing.

A few aquatic species are also known, such as *O. disticha* which grows in temporary pools during winter. The leaves and flowers float on the surface until the pool dries up in summer and appear again as it fills the following winter.

195. *Oxalis obtusa*

96. *Oxalis purpurea*

200. *Oxalis smithiana:* Rooisuring

97. *Oxalis tenella*

98. *Oxalis heidelbergensis*

201. *Oxalis polyphylla:* Vingersuring

99. *Oxalis luteola*

202. *Oxalis disticha*

203. *Monsonia speciosa:* Butterfly flower, Slangblom

204. *Pelargonium incarnatum*

GERANIACEAE

Almost half the known species which comprise the Geraniaceae are to be found in South Africa. Their characteristic fruits are an unmistakable family feature and have inspired several of the Greek-derived generic names such as *Geranium* (crane's bill), *Pelargonium* (stork's bill) and *Erodium* (heron's bill). This allusion to birds' beaks is at once apparent if one examines the developing, pointed fruits. When ripe, the whole structure splits into five segments, explosively catapulting the seeds into the air for dispersal. *Geranium* itself is represented here by almost 18 species of which the best known in *G. incanum*, often seen along Southern Cape roads. *Geranium* and its other allies shown on this page are readily distinguished by having five petals of equal size whereas the *Pelargonium* does not.

Monsonia speciosa in pink, white or creamy-green tones is a handsome tuberous perennial which enlivens gravelly hills and flats in the Western Cape during spring. A sensitive deep-seated tuberous root system makes it a difficult and capricious species in cultivation.

Sarcocaulon is a shrubby genus mainly from the arid western regions of the Cape. They are commonly called Bushman's candles because their thick resinous stems are highly inflammable, blazing furiously if set alight.

205. *Sarcocaulon multifidum*

206. *Sarcocaulon herrei*

207. *Sarcocaulon patersonii:* Candlebush, Boesmanskers

208. *Monsonia speciosa:* Butterfly flower, Slangblom

209. *Geranium incanum:* Vrouebossie, Bergtee

210. *Sarcocaulon crassicaule:* Candlebush, Boesmansdoring

211. *Sarcocaulon l'heritieri*

PELARGONIUM

There is little doubt that the genus *Pelargonium* is South Africa's greatest contribution to the world's gardens. With more than 250 species indigenous here, this genus is the largest and most important in the Geraniaceae. Incidentally, the so-called 'geraniums' are in fact hybrids between various species of *Pelargonium*.

The scarlet-flowered *P. inquinans* and the pink *P. salmoneum* and *P. zonale* – all from the Eastern Cape bush – have contributed to the parentage of modern garden or zonal 'geraniums'.

Similarly, *P. peltatum* from the Eastern Cape Province is the ancestor of the so-called 'ivy-leaved geraniums'.

These are some of the herbaceous or shrubby species, but in Namaqualand and in the Karoo many bizarre growth forms have been evolved. Some are tuberous with large turnip-like rootstocks, growing in winter and dying down in summer. Others have developed swollen succulent stems or are covered with spines. In high mountainous areas species such as *P. tricolor* from the Swartberg and also the Langeberg at Riversdale have a dwarf, tufted, almost alpine mode of growth. Indeed, in *Pelargonium* we see how a group of plants has diversified, evolved and adapted to the many ecological niches available to it.

212. *Pelargonium tricolor*

213. *Pelargonium inquinans*: Scarlet pelargonium, Wilde malva

215. *Pelargonium triste*: Kaneelblom

214. *Pelargonium oreophilum*

216. *Pelargonium hermanniifolium*

217. *Pelargonium peltatum*

218. *Pelargonium betulinum:* Birch-leaf pelargonium, Kanferblaar, Maagpynbossie, Suurbos

219. *Pelargonium cucullatum:* Hooded-leaf pelargonium, Tree pelargonium, Wilde malva

220. *Pelargonium magenteum*

221. *Pelargonium karooicum*

EUPHORBIACEAE

uphorbias are found throughout the world in an amazing range of life forms from tropical trees to tiny annual herbs, but in South Africa they are nearly all succulents. *E. meloformis* is an extreme form from the Eastern Cape Province, reduced to a globe-like body, while others such as *E. cooperi* from Mpumalanga and KwaZulu-Natal are large and tree-like. All euphorbias have latex canals in their tissues so that when leaves or stems are cut a milky juice at once flows from the wound. Usually this latex is severely irritant but certain species like *E. virosa* from near the Orange River mouth produce highly toxic latex, so toxic that it was used by the San as an ingredient in their arrow-poisons.

Most of our euphorbias are stem-succulents, that is, their stems are green and swollen, filled with water-storing tissues, but their leaves are either vestigial or soon drop off. Only in a few species such as *E. hamata* from the Clanwilliam district do some leaves persist for any length of time. In this species they often become suffused with red pigments. Sometimes succulent euphorbias' stems are tightly compressed and so the adult plant grows to form a hard mound as is seen in *E. pulvinata* from the Eastern Cape Province. A similar but looser growth habit is seen in *E. caput-medusae* from the West Coast, so named because its lax, contorted stems resemble the writhing snakes on the head of the Gorgon, Medusa.

222. *Euphorbia meloformis:* Eselkos, Bobbejaankos, Skilpadkos

223. *Euphorbia caput-medusae:* Medusa's head, Vingerpol

224. *Euphorbia virosa:* Boesmansgif

225. *Euphorbia esculenta:* Soetvingerpol

226. *Euphorbia ledienii:* Noorsdoring, Suurnoors

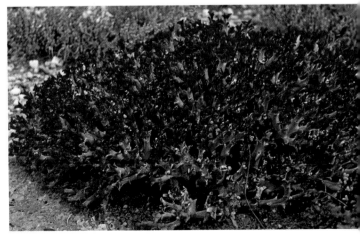

227. *Euphorbia hamata:* Olifantsmelkbos

228. *Euphorbia pulvinata:* Pincushion, Voetangel

229. *Euphorbia caput-medusae:* Medusa's head, Vingerpol

230. *Euphorbia grandicornis:* Transvaal candelabra tree

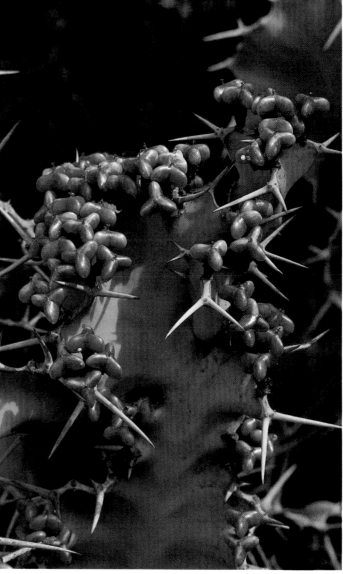

231. *Euphorbia cooperi:* Transvaalse kandelaarnaboom

RUTACEAE

It is not easy to associate the familiar tropical Asian members of this family belonging to the genus *Citrus* with their largely heath-like South African relatives; yet a common factor – the presence of numerous volatile-oil-producing glands on their vegetative parts – is an easily recognizable unifying feature. However, *Calodendrum capense*, a beautiful tree of our evergreen forests producing chestnut-like fruits, does bear some resemblance to its tropical relatives.

Nevertheless, the Rutaceae in South Africa are concentrated mainly in the Western Cape Province where *Agathosma* and *Adenandra* are important genera. All are heathy, strongly aromatic shrubs to which a generalized name, buchu, is often applied. Real buchu, *Agathosma crenulata* and oval-leaved buchu, *Agathosma betulina*, were used as blood purifiers even before the advent of Western man at the Cape, and are still extensively prescribed in herbal remedies for kidney complaints. *Adenandra villosa* is one of the larger flowered, more ornamental species which in general are known more for their foliar fragrance than floral splendour.

232. *Calodendrum capense:* Cape chestnut, Wildekastaiing

233. *Adenandra villosa:* China flower, Betsie

POLYGALACEAE

The Polygalaceae or milkwort family frequently gives rise to some confusion among non-botanists because the flower has a superficial resemblance to those of the pea-flowered legumes. *Polygala* itself is cosmopolitan, comprising some 600 species, with about 100 in South Africa. *P. virgata* and *P. myrtifolia*, both from the Cape, are attractive shrubs occasionally seen in cultivation, but few of our other species are especially noteworthy. Most polygalas have purple flowers but in *Nylandtia*, a related genus endemic to the Cape, white forms occasionally appear. *Nylandtia* is also unusual in that after flowering, instead of dry seeds, it produces a copy of juicy edible berries. these bright orange berries are called 'skilpadbessies' and are much loved by children and birds alike.

The name *Polygala* means 'much milk', alluding to an ancient but unsubstantiated belief that cows increase their milk yields if allowed to browse on these plants. However, the powdered roots of several local species are prescribed as a purgative and vermifuge by Zulu herbalists.

236. *Nylandtia spinosa:* Duinbessie, Skilpadbessie

237. *Polygala virgata:* Bloukappie

234. *Nylandtia spinosa:* Duinbessie, Skilpadbessie

235. *Polygala myrtifolia*: Septemberbossie, Blouertjieboom

238. *Polygala bracteolaris*

ICACINACEAE

Although popularly called white pear, *Apodytes dimidiata* is in no way related to the familiar table fruit of that name but was probably so called because its pale timber closely resembles pear wood. In the 19th century Cape wagon builders prized this timber for its tough elastic qualities. Although found in almost all temperate evergreen forests from the Cape Peninsula to Ethiopia, *Apodytes dimidiata* is not particularly distinctive except when in fruit. That stage is shown here with a cluster of ripe black seeds and their bright orange supporting arils.

AITONIACEAE

Chinese lantern tree and 'klapperbossie' are both appropriate and familiar names for this very decorative little tree which enlivens the Little Karoo's landscape in winter and spring. As spring and early summer advance, its comparatively dull pink flowers fade, giving way to plump crimson suffused pods. Many gardeners have unsuccessfully attempted to grow *Nymania capensis*: it will only flourish in arid or semi-arid areas. A small-leaved form is found in the Northern Cape Province.

239. *Apodytes dimidiata:* White pear, Witpeer

240. *Nymania capensis:* Chinese lanterns, Klapperbos

SAPINDACEAE

This family is closely related to the Aitoniaceae and indeed the Namaqualand red balloon, *Erythrophysa alata*, a small shrub from rocky koppies in the Northern Cape Province, is often mistaken for *Nymania*. *Erythrophysa* is easily recognized by its compound leaves; *Nymania* has simple leaves.

BOMBACACEAE

The baobab, *Adansonia digitata*, is probably Africa's most famous tree. In our country it grows only in warm, dry parts of the Northern Province and Mpumalanga, ranging as far south as the Soutpansberg and Olifants River.

Its huge, white, sweetly scented flowers, believed to be pollinated by bats, precede large egg-shaped pods. When broken open these pods reveal numerous seeds embedded in a spongy white pulp with a faint flavour reminiscent of sherbert – hence the baobab's other popular name, cream-of-tartar tree.

Animals often chew baobab stems to relieve their thirst in times of drought because, despite its massive bulky trunk, the tissues of *Adansonia* are soft, pulpy and rather watery.

TILIACEAE

Sparrmannia africana, commonly called the Cape stock rose, belongs to the jute family, a group of plants noted for the commercial importance of their fibres. Many years ago attempts were made to exploit *Sparrmannia* fibres commercially in the Storms River area but their quality failed to match that of Asian jute and the project was abandoned. Nevertheless, it is a most decorative soft-wooded tree – an old favourite as a tub plant in Victorian conservatories. It is frequently seen along streams and forest margins between George and Humansdorp, flowering in early winter.

241. *Erythrophysa alata:* Namaqualand red balloon

242. *Sparrmannia africana:* Cape stock rose, Kaapse stokroos

243. *Adansonia digitata:* Baobab, Kremetartboom

RHAMNACEAE

There are some 150 species of *Phylica* in South Africa, mainly concentrated in the Western Cape Province where they are important constituents of fynbos vegetation. Their flowers are so tiny that they must be viewed through a hand-lens. But they are amply compensated for such diminutive flowers by the presence of numerous feathery to silky sub-tending bracts in white, pink, grey or golden shades which in certain species render each flowerhead quite spectacularly conspicuous. Phylicas are mainly shrubs or small trees, especially prominent in dry, mountainous country like the Cedarberg and Koue Bokkeveld.

244. *Phylica marlothii*

245. *Phylica dodii*

246. *Phylica stipularis:* Hondegesiggie

247. *Phylica pubescens:* Featherhead, Veerkoppie

248. *Phylica rigida*

GREYIACEAE

There are only three species of *Greyia* in the world and they are all from South Africa. Some botanists assign them to the family Melianthaceae but many classify them in a distinct, exclusively South African family known as Greyiaceae. These soft-wooded shrubs or small trees from the Eastern Cape Province, KwaZulu-Natal and Mpumalanga are rather similar in appearance, producing, in late winter and early spring, masses of dense, scarlet flower-spikes at the tips of their bare branches. *Greyia sutherlandii* – Natal bottle-brush – is the best-known species, for it is such a conspicuous feature of crags or forest margins in the KwaZulu-Natal Drakensberg and is also finding its way into more and more private gardens as a decorative ornamental.

249. *Greyia sutherlandii:* Natal bottlebrush

250. *Greyia sutherlandii:* Natal bottlebrush

MALVACEAE

Hibiscus, the largest genus of the mallow family, comprises some 300 species of which at least 50 are found in South Africa. Some are diminutive herbs like *Hibiscus trionum* while others like *Hibiscus tiliaceus*, a coastal species from KwaZulu-Natal, grow into six-metre-tall trees. *Hibiscus tiliaceus*, often found associated with mangrove swamps, is the source of a useful fibre for making ropes, sails and fishing nets in sub-tropical and tropical areas bordering the Indian Ocean.

A distinctive feature of this family is that the stamens are united to form a tubular column in the centre of each flower.

251. *Hibiscus vitifolius:* Hibiscus, Wildestokroos

252. *Hibiscus aethiopicus*

253. *Hibiscus pedunculatus:* Hibiscus, Wildestokroos

254. *Hibiscus pusillus*

255. *Hibiscus tiliaceus:* Wild cotton tree, Wilde katoenboom

256. *Pavonia columella*

257. *Hibiscus trionum:* Black-eyed Susan, Terblanzbossie

STERCULIACEAE

This largely tropical to sub-tropical family of woody plants has many decorative representatives in South Africa. Of the several species of *Dombeya* that are found in KwaZulu-Natal, the Northern Province and Mpumalanga, *Dombeya burgessiae*, a pretty pink-and-white flowered shrub from the Lowveld, is now grown in many private gardens; while the so-called wild pear, *Dombeya rotundifolia* from the Bushveld, is without doubt one of the most spectacular trees found in South Africa. During late winter and spring the bare branches of this tree are covered with beautiful, pure white blooms – an unforgettable display when seen against a dusty brown bushveld landscape.

Trees of the genus *Sterculia* – popularly called lowveld chestnuts – are known not so much for their flowers as for their seed pods. After these hard, woody pods have split open and released their seeds, they are often collected for use in dried flower arrangements.

But *Hermannia*, with some 200 species in South Africa, is by far the most important genus of this family in our region. Hermannias are found in arid and semi-arid environments, and are especially common in the Karoo where they are prominent among the Little Karoo bushes which, in that desolate area, so miraculously sustain great flocks of sheep. Most hermannias have insignificant yellow flowers, but a few such as *H. stricta* are a lovely sight when in full bloom.

258. *Dombeya rotundifolia:* Common wild pear, Gewone drolpeer

59. *Dombeya burgessiae:* Pink wild pear (white form), Persdrolpeer

260. *Hermannia stricta:* Rooi-opslag

261. *Sterculia rogersii:* Common star chestnut, Gewone sterkastaiing

62. *Sterculia rogersii:* Common star chestnut, Gewone sterkastaiing

263. *Sterculia murex:* Lowveld chestnut, Laeveld kastaiing

PENAEACEAE

The Penaeaceae is one of several plant families to be found only in South Africa. This small but very distinct family consists of 27 species, all endemic to the Western Cape Province. They are found mainly in mountainous country, growing almost exclusively on poor sandy soils derived from Table Mountain sandstone.

Most species are characterised by their very restricted distribution ranges. *Brachysiphon imbri-* *catus*, for example, grows only on the Cape Peninsula while *Endonema retzioides* has an even more limited range in the Riviersonderend Mountains. But by far the most restricted of all is *Glischrocolla formosa*, an exceptionally rare shrublet known from only a few stands in the Franschhoek and Hottentots Holland mountains. One of the rarest Cape plants, it was discovered in 1790 by Francis Masson, plant collector to the

264. *Saltera sarcocolla:* Vlieëbos

Royal Botanic Gardens at Kew, who gathered specimens in the Franschhoek Mountains: but no further specimens were seen until 1932 when Thomas Stokoe found a small colony in the Hottentots Holland Mountains above Somerset West.

Fortunately, *Saltera sarcocolla*, the most attractive member of the family, is fairly widespread from the Cape Peninsula to Bredasdorp. It shows the family's characteristic floral structure of a colourful four-lobed calyx tube with no petals. *Saltera* is very variable in form and colour, with both pink and white, long and short tubed variations found within a single species.

Most Penaeaceae are small heath-like shrubs growing in open veld, but a few such as *Sonderothamnus petraeus* are rock dwellers, surviving quite happily rooted in bare rock crevices.

265. *Saltera sarcocolla:* Vlieëbos

266. *Sonderothamnus petraeus*

67. *Glischrocolla formosa*

68. *Endonema retzioides*

269. *Brachysiphon imbricatus:* Sissies

THYMELAEACEAE

The Thymelaeaceae or Daphne family is cosmopolitan in its range, but especially abundant in South Africa where the majority of species are centred in the Western Cape Province. *Gnidia* (100 species) and *Struthiola* (40 species) are the largest genera. An important family character is that the calyx is a brightly-coloured tube, while the petals are usually reduced to dull inconspicuous scales at the mouth of the calyx tube. Another unmistakable character is the exceedingly tough bard which splits longitudinally into fibrous strips like rope strands. Most South African Thymelaeaceae are common components of the Cape fynbos where they are generally small heath-like shrubs, but a few, such as *Gnidia kraussiana* found over much of the interior of South Africa, are more widespread. This latter species is commonly called 'gifbossie', for it is exceedingly poisonous to domestic stock – a mere handful of leaves is enough to kill a horse or a cow.

Lachnaea, the 'bergasters', are handsome shrubs from high altitudes in the Cape mountains but few have ever been successfully cultivated. Fortunately the pompon tree, *Dais cotinifolia*, has adapted well to cultivation and is now grown throughout South Africa and in many other warm parts of the world. It is one of the few trees in this family and is found in the eastern parts of the country between East London and the Northern Province.

270. *Lachnaea filamentosa:* Bergaster

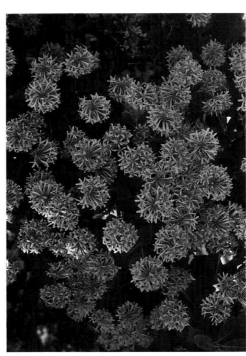

271. *Dais cotinifolia:* Pompon tree

272. *Lachnaea buxifolia*

273. *Gnidia kraussiana:* Gifbossie

274. *Struthiola dodecandra:*
Katstertjie, Soetgonna

275. *Gnidia penicillata*

276. *Gnidia tomentosa*

277. *Gnidia polycephala:* Besembos, Januariebos

FLACOURTIACEAE

There are only a few representatives of this essentially tropical family in our region. All are woody shrubs and most of them have insignificant flowers. However, *Xylotheca kraussiana* – aptly named the African dogrose (although it is in no way related to true roses) – is an exception. This evergreen shrub or small tree grows in coastal forests in KwaZulu-Natal. Its fragrant white flowers are followed by large woody seed capsules, filled with striking black and red seeds.

278. *Xylotheca kraussiana:* African dogrose, Afrikaanse hondsroos

PASSIFLORACEAE

To this family belongs the granadilla or passion fruit, a delicious South American representative of the family, so familiar on fruit stalls and in gardens in many parts of the world.

However, the African Passifloraceae, unlike their transatlantic cousins, have a sinister reputation; despite its alluring fruits, *Adenia digitata* is virulently poisonous. Several human fatalities have been reported from the Northern Province, Mpumalanga, KwaZulu-Natal and Botswana, where this tuberous-rooted vine occurs naturally. Death usually follows a few hours after eating the tempting fruits. There are some nine other species of *Adenia* in South Africa and all should be avoided. They have massive turnip-like rootstocks from which trailing stems emerge with the onset of the summer rains. Small, dull-coloured tubular flowers are produced in early summer followed by the colourful fruits, shown here.

Adenias are today much sought after by collectors of succulents who prize the grotesque forms of their bloated rootstocks.

279. *Adenia digitata:* Bobbejaangif

CUCURBITACEAE

Even non-botanists can hardly fail to recognize members of the Cucurbitaceae – the pumpkin, cucumber and marrow family. Cucurbits are difficult to classify because their flowers are so similar but their fruits show great diversity and more often than not are the most reliable means of identification. They are mostly annual trailing vines, germinating with the onset of summer rains, flowering and then producing their fruits in autumn.

Acanthosicyos naudiniana, a type of wild cucumber or 'tsamma', is common in the Northern Cape Province. It is an important water source for the San who also roast the pips and then grind them up to form an edible meal.

Cucumis africanus is found in many other dry parts of South Africa as well as in the Eastern Cape Province. Like other members of the family this species is also edible but should be treated with caution as bitter-tasting mutants occasionally appear containing a poisonous principle which can be harmful.

In warmer sub-tropical areas like KwaZulu-Natal, the genus *Momordica* predominates. Momordicas are usually climbers, scrambling amongst shrubs or over bushes and other plants with their fruits draped among the branches, creating a beautiful display. The Zulu use an infusion of *Momordica involucrata* as a sedative for an upset stomach.

280. *Acanthosicyos naudiniana:* Tsamma, Wildekomkommer

281. *Cucumis africanus:* Wild cucumber

282. *Cucumis metuliferus:* Rooi-agurkie, Wildekomkommer

LECYTHIDACEAE

B*arringtonia racemosa* is the only member of the Lecythidaceae in South Africa, where it is popularly called the powder-puff tree. Like the other 38 Indo-Pacific species of *Barringtonia*, *B. racemosa* is also a mangrove. It can be found in most warm, humid areas bordering the Indian and Pacific oceans, extending down the East African coast to KwaZulu-Natal. Mangrove is a term used to describe trees of various families which have adapted to life on coastal mudflats, estuaries or inlets in the tropics. They are subjected to salty inundations with every high tide but have evolved various methods of surviving this exposure, such as breathing roots which stand clear of the high water mark.

In *B. racemosa*, large oval seeds follow the delicate powder-puff-like flowers. Each seed is enclosed in a light spongy casing giving it a high degree of buoyancy. When mature they fall to the mud below and then float away on the next high tide. Germination follows almost immediately. Soon the floating seed anchors itself and at once begins to grow into a new tree.

283. *Barringtonia racemosa:* Powder-puff tree, Poeierkwasboom

284. A mangrove setting with *Avicennia marina* (Verbenaceae) and seedlings of *Bruguiera gymnorrhiza* (Rhizophoraceae)

MELASTOMACEAE

Several exotic South American species of *Tibouchina* and *Lasiandra* are commonly grown in many of our gardens, so this pan-tropical family is generally fairly familiar in South Africa. But only a few members of the Melastomaceae are actually indigenous to this country where they are found in the warmer, moister parts of Mpumalanga or along the KwaZulu-Natal coast. The curiously jointed stamens are a distinctive feature of the family.

Dissotis, an African genus of some 140 species, is represented in South Africa by only five different species. *Dissotis princeps*, a large-flowered shrub, is particularly common in swampy ground along the KwaZulu-Natal coast. The smaller-flowered *Dissotis canescens* occurs on the Mpumalanga escarpment.

Purple, pink and pure white colour forms of *Dissotis princeps* are known. It is especially suited to cultivation in wet boggy soil and grows surprisingly well at Kirstenbosch where it makes a fine, colourful display in February.

Dissotis canescens has smaller flowers of a clear rosy pink.

285. *Dissotis canescens*: Ordeal bean

286. *Dissotis princeps*: Kalwerbossie   287. *Dissotis princeps*: Kalwerbossie   288. *Dissotis princeps*: Kalwerbossie

COMBRETACEAE

Combretums are found in almost all the warmer parts of the world, except Australia. In Africa they are especially abundant and are very conspicuous in the savannas. *Terminalia* (seven species) and *Combretum* (30 species) are our largest genera. Nearly all are trees or shrubs with rather dull insignificant flowers but very decorative four-winged, angular seed pods. *Combretum microphyllum* is exceptional in that it is a rampant scrambler, covered with great sprays of scarlet flowers in summer. This lovely creeper is found in hot valleys in the Lowveld in Mpumalanga. Its gorgeous blooms are followed in autumn by clusters of pinkish, angular fruits, equally attractive in their own right.

289. *Combretum microphyllum*

290. *Combretum microphyllum:* Flame creeper, Vlamklimop

ERICACEAE

Erica is the largest genus of flowering plants in South Africa. Well over 657 species are found in this country while there are probably many more as yet undescribed. Heaths do occur in other parts of the world such as the East African highlands, around the Mediterranean basin and in Western Europe – amounting to some 28 species – but the occurrence of over 625 species all massed in the South Western Cape Province remains a botanical mystery. On the Cape Peninsula alone there are 103 species of *Erica*.

No other group of plants is more important a component of fynbos vegetation than the heaths. There is scarcely a habitat to which they have not been able to adapt. Ericas grow on coastal headlands, open flats, in bare rock crevices, along streamsides, in boggy swamps

291. *Erica blenna:* Lantern heath

292. *Erica corydalis:* White petticoat heath

293. *Erica decora:* Sticky rose heath

294. *Erica densifolia:* Sticky red-and-green heath, Knysnaheide

295. *Erica fastigiata* and *Moraea fugax*

296. *Erica mammosa:* Nine-pin heath, Rooiklossieheide

297. *Erica longiflora*

298. *Erica junonia*

and on the summits of our highest peaks. They flower throughout the year, with a different species coming into bloom almost every week. Indeed, one can take a walk in the Cape mountains any day of the year and find several different heaths in full bloom. Few other plant groups can match such seasonal and floral diversity.

Ericas take many different shapes and colours. The large, long-tubed species are among the most striking, like *E. mammosa* and *E. dichrus*. Both are robust species which have become popular garden subjects.

299. *Erica decora* and *Leucadendron laureolum*

300. *Erica dichrus*

301. *Erica viscaria:* Sticky heath, Klokkiesheide

Not all heaths take easily to cultivation, especially those from the summits of high mountains such as the graceful, long-necked *E. junonia*. This rarity from the Koue Bokkeveld Mountains has proved difficult to grow away from its natural habitat.

This page gives some idea of the great floral diversity of Cape heaths. It is hardly surprising that early botanical explorers were entranced by these charming little shrubs and soon introduced them to great private collections. During the late 18th and early 19th centuries the cult of growing Cape heaths in Europe reached its climax. The then Duke of Bedford had several hundred species in cultivation by 1800. In recent years there has been a revival of interest in ericas, and many South Africans now grow them in their own gardens.

303. *Erica fastigiata:* Four sisters heath

302. *Erica curviflora:* Waterbos

304. *Erica melanthera*

05. *Erica onosmaeflora*

306. *Erica bruniades:* Kapokkie

07. *Erica massonii:* Houw Hoek heath, Taaiheide

308. *Erica tegulaefolia:* Banketheide

309. *Erica ventricosa:* Washeide, Franschhoekheide

GENTIANACEAE

In Europe members of this cosmopolitan family usually have vivid blue flowers such as the famous blue gentians of the Alps, but in South Africa they are only pink, yellow or white.

These rather delicate annual or perennial herbs are found mainly in the moister parts of the country. *Chironia* (15 species) and *Sebaea* (41 species) are the largest South African genera.

A few species do grow at high elevations, and indeed *Sebaea thodeana* from the Drakensberg and Lesotho is somewhat reminiscent of certain European gentians except for its colour.

Some species have adapted to more arid situations such as *Orphium frutescens*, a woody shrublet which grows in brackish soils in coastal areas and has exquisite pink flowers that appear to be sculpted from wax.

311. *Orphium frutescens:* Teeringbos

310. *Sebaea exacoides:* Naeltjiesblom

312. *Chironia linoides* subspecies *emarginata*

313. *Sebaea thodeana*

14. *Plumbago auriculata:* Plumbago, Syselbos

PLUMBAGINACEAE

Blue *Plumbago auriculata* is said to have been the favourite flower of Cecil Rhodes. It is a native of the Eastern Cape Province, KwaZulu-Natal and Mpumalanga, where it grows as a straggling shrub or scrambler. But in cultivation, with clipping and shaping, it can soon be coaxed to form one of the most beautiful formal hedges one could wish for. It is almost always pale blue but rare white-flowered mutants are occasionally encountered.

Limonium perigrinum, the largest of our sea lavenders, is common in coastal bush along the West Coast near Saldanha Bay. These are among the hardiest members of the family, well able to survive prolonged droughts as well as brackish soil yet producing masses of papery pink blooms each year without fail.

15. *Plumbago auriculata:* Plumbago, Syselbos

316. *Limonium perigrinum:* Sea lavender, Strandroos, Papierblom

OLEACEAE

Most non-botanists do not associate olives and jasmine, yet they both belong to the same plant family. In South Africa there are four indigenous olives (though none is large enough to eat), and ten indigenous jasmines. *Jasminum multipartitum* is the most decorative of our native species. It has large flowers and is endowed with a delicious fragrance. This handsome evergreen shrub is found on dry koppies or in scrub and bush throughout the Eastern Cape Province, KwaZulu-Natal and parts of Mpumalanga. It is being grown in more and more gardens, often displacing the familiar domesticated Asiatic jasmines.

317. *Jasminum multipartitum:* Wild jasmine

APOCYNACEAE

Most members of this family are found in the tropics where they are usually evergreen trees, shrubs or climbers, but in South Africa, especially in warmer drier areas, they are often stem succulents. A good example is the impala lily, *Adenium multiflorum*, familiar to all visitors to the Kruger Park. Its magnificent blooms are produced during winter and early spring in clusters at the tips of fleshy, swollen stems.

In North Western Namaqualand *Pachypodium namaquanum* adopts a similar mode of growth in response to arid environmental conditions. Cylindrical trunks – only rarely branched – are topped by clusters of leaves during the brief winter growing period. Namaqualanders call this weird tree 'halfmens' because, when seen in silhouette against an evening skyline, it seems like a ghostly human apparition. Avaricious succulent collectors have long prized the bizarre 'halfmens' which today is officially classed as an endangered species. Large specimens reach great ages: the one seen here is probably well over one hundred years old.

Whether succulent or shrubby, most Apocynaceae have milky white sap, and many are characterized by the presence of poisonous alkaloids in the tissue. Consequently, members of this family are best treated as poisonous, but there are exceptions such as the genus *Carissa* which bears edible fruits.

318. *Carissa macrocarpa*: Natal plum, Amatungulu, Grootnoem-noem,

319. *Pachypodium namaquanum*: Elephant's trunk, Halfmens

320. *Adenium multiflorum:* Impala lily, Impalalelie

321. *Stapelia flavopurpurea*

322. *Duvalia reclinata:* Hottentotstoontjie, Kabietjie

ASCLEPIADACEAE

Shrubby and herbaceous members of this great tropical to sub-tropical family are commonly called milkweeds because of an abundance of milky latex in their sap. *Pachycarpus*, a herbaceous grassland genus from KwaZulu-Natal, the Northern Province and Mpumalanga, is a typical example.

In South Africa, however, the tribe Stapeliae is dominant. These are stem succulents with watery rather than milky sap, varying in size from metre-high genera like *Hoodia* to miniature forms such as *Duvalia* and *Huernia*. They have evolved some of the most exotic and architecturally bizarre flowers in the plant kingdom with some of the most complex floral structures and equally complex pollination mechanisms. Most stapeliad flowers give off strongly fetid odours on opening, recalling various forms of organic decay. Attracted by these odours bluebottles and other flies swarm over the open blooms and in so doing pick up pollen and transfer it to another flower. Pollen is formed in two tiny waxy sacs linked by a yoke-like arm, which hooks in a fly's foot and is then transported to another flower of the same species where it slots perfectly into a stigmatic groove. The 'fit' varies from species to species but is so precise as to be a 'lock and key' mechanism. If pollination is effected, two V-shaped pods are formed rather like the horns of a goat, and so many country folk call stapeliads 'bokhorinkies'. An old Khoikhoi word 'ghaap' is also currently used but refers more specifically to edible species. In Namaqualand their fleshy angular stems are still eaten fresh, pickled or preserved in syrup.

323. *Huernia zebrina*

324. *Pachycarpus grandiflorus*

325. *Hoodia macrantha:* Wildeghaap

326. *Hoodia flava:* Ghaap

327. *Huerniopsis decipiens:* Kalkoennetjie

328. *Quaqua armata:* Aroena

329. *Microloma tenuifolium:* Wax creeper, Kannetjies

330. *Stapelia grandiflora:* Slangghaap

331. *Pachycarpus scaber*

332. *Quaqua inversa*

333. *Brachystelma barberae:* Platvoetaasblom

Other members of the family are tuberous-rooted like *Microloma*, the wax creeper which annually develops twining stems from an underground rootstock. *Brachystelma*, which grows chiefly in summer-rainfall areas, has enormous turnip-like tubers from which clusters of elegantly geometric flowers are produced in spring and summer.

334. *Orbeopsis lutea*

CONVOLVULACEAE

Twiners, creepers and climbers predominate in this large family which is found in most parts of the world except the coldest regions. It is well developed in South Africa where about 120 species grow naturally.

Ipomoea, the largest genus, is cosmopolitan, with some 50 species in our area. Commonly called morning glories, their garishly coloured but delicate flowers open mainly in the cool of the early morning. As the day wears on they wither, collapsing by evening, to be followed by another flower the next day. *Ipomoea crassipes* is a grassland species from the Eastern Cape Province and KwaZulu-Natal. It is valued by certain African tribes for its alleged magical

335. *Merremia kentrocaulos*

336. *Ipomoea pellita*

properties: the powdered root is used as a love charm or to prevent harm befalling a village. Ground-up roots are fed by the Zulu to their cattle if they wish to prevent anyone harming them.

While South African ipomoeas are predominantly pink or mauve-flowered, *Merremia* is a genus of white, cream or yellow-flowered climbers. *Merremia kentrocaulos* has a wide range in central and southern Africa. It is frequently seen in parts of the Northern Province and Mpumalanga during summer, either forming prostrate mats at the roadside or climbing to a height of 10 metres if suitable trees are available. Bushveld areas, especially the Kruger Park, are favoured habitats.

337. *Ipomoea crassipes*

338. *Lobostemon glaucophyllus*

BORAGINACEAE

The borage or forget-me-not family is a large, distinctive group of plants, mainly of herbs and shrubs, found throughout the world but especially in Mediterranean regions. Their flowers are predominantly blue and their vegetative parts are invariably covered with characteristic stiff hairs or bristles. In South Africa *Lobostemon* the largest genus, consisting of some 30 species, is centred in the Western Cape Province and Namaqualand. Lobostemons are tough, drought-resistant shrubs found principally in semi-arid regions.

339. *Lobostemon fruticosus:* Luibossie, Agtdaegeneesbos

340. *Lobostemon montanus*

Lobostemon fruticosus is the most common and colourful species. It is locally abundant on dry hillsides in the South Western Cape Province, becoming very conspicuous for a few brief weeks in spring when it is covered in blooms ranging from pinkish-mauve through almost every imaginable hue of blue. Superior colour forms would be ornamental in gardens in dry regions yet, strangely, have never been introduced into cultivation.

'Agtdaegeneesbos' (eight-day healing bush) is a common name applied to *L. fruticosus* and other lobostemons. This quaint name was coined by early colonists who used an infusion of the leaves to wash body sores and other skin eruptions such as ringworm. The salve was thought to bring about healing within eight days.

LAMIACEAE (LABIATAE)

Mint, sage, thyme and lavender all belong to the large economically important family, the Lamiaceae (or Labiatae as it is alternatively called). However, apart from a few indigenous mints (*Mentha* species), no important culinary herbs are found among the South African representatives, although the colourful ornamentals in this family are legion.

In this country the family appears to be centred in the Northern Province and Mpumalanga. Aromatic foliage and quadrangular stems are obvious identifying characters. Almost every one of the approximately 50 species of *Plectranthus* is worth cultivating. *Plectranthus ecklonii* and *P. fruticosus* are already established garden plants, as is *Leonotis leonurus* – rather confusingly known as wild dagga. Apparently possessing mild narcotic properties but not related to true dagga (*Cannabis*), this splendid garden plant is common in many parts of the country, usually in its orange form. Creamy-white mutations are also cultivated.

The beautiful, diminutive-flowered *Tetradenia riparia* blooms towards the end of winter in a bare, leafless condition, making a most striking display. It is frequent in Mpumalanga and also KwaZulu-Natal where the Zulu make infusions of the leaves to cure respiratory complaints. Pychnostachys urticifolia, notable for its vivid blue flowers, is a tall perennial reaching as much as three metres in height in its natural habitat, the Northern Province.

341. *Leonotis leonurus:* Wild dagga, Duiwelstabak

342. *Pychnostachys urticifolia*

343. *Plectranthus ecklonii*

344. *Leonotis leonurus:* Wild dagga, Duiwelstabak

345. *Hemizygia foliosa*

346. *Orthosiphon labiatus*

347. *Plectranthus fruticosus:* Muishondblaar

348. *Tetradenia riparia:* Iboza, Watersalie

SCROPHULARIACEAE

This large cosmopolitan family has contributed innumerable fine ornamentals to our gardens, many of them South African plants.

Nemesia strumosa, a multicoloured annual from the Darling sandveld, a few kilometres north of Cape Town, is now cultivated worldwide. Despite a very restricted distribution range, there are several naturally occurring colour forms, each peculiar to a specific locality: so plant breeders have had little need to improve on what nature originally provided.

Phygelius capensis, a woody perennial from high cold parts of the Eastern Cape Province and Drakensberg, is one of the few South African plants sufficiently hardy to thrive outdoors in Britain.

In arid regions, especially the Karoo, various species of *Aptosimum* are encountered. These small tufted shrublets survive long periods of desiccation, but after good spring rains they are covered with flowers of a quite startlingly vivid blue.

There are also several parasitic genera in this family. *Cycnium adonense* from KwaZulu-Natal and Mpumalanga is a partial parasite, drawing somewhat on its host's resources but still able to photosynthesize through its own green leaves. But *Harveya* and *Hyobanche*, both Cape-centred genera, have no green leaves of their own and are total parasites, attached to their hosts' root systems through which they draw all their sustenance.

349 *Cycnium adonense:* Mushroom flower

350. *Harveya capensis:* Inkblom

351. *Zaluzianskya microsiphon*

352. *Nemesia strumosa:* Leeubekkie

353. *Nemesia macroceras*

357. *Phygelius capensis*

354. *Hyobanche sanguinea:* Snail flower, Aardroos

355. *Aptosimum procumbens:* Wild violet, Brandblare

356. *Diascia longicornis:* Pensies

358. *Harveya squamosa*

359. *Harveya bolusii:* Inkblom

360. *Dicerocaryum eriocarpum:* Devil's thorn, Beesdubbeltjie

PEDALIACEAE

The Pedaliaceae is a small family of plants found principally in Africa with a few outliers found in regions such as Australia and Indo-Malaysia. At least half are indigenous to South Africa.

Sesamum, the largest genus, is well known as a source of oil-rich edible seeds – the popular sesame seeds often seen sprinkled on loaves of bread. Obtained from an Indian species, *S. indicum*, there seems no reason why seeds from any of its approximately 23 indigenous species (especially *S. capense*) should not be equally good if appropriately selected.

Ceratotheca triloba, a common summer-flowering annual in the Northern Province and Mpumalanga, is often confused with *S. capense*. Both look very much like the foxglove but *Ceratotheca* has sharp spines on the valves of its seed capsule while *Sesamum* does not. This trend towards the development of spines on the seed capsules is very obvious in South African Pedaliaceae; evidently an adaptation to dispersal by animals. *Dicerocaryum eriocarpum*, a trailing creeper from Mpumalanga, has stud-like fruits armed with powerful twin spines, like an outsized double-pronged thumbtack. They are picked up on the feet of grazing animals and carried considerable distances.

When immersed in water, the stems and leaves of *Dicerocaryum* give off quantities of soapy mucilage and this species was in fact used as a soap substitute during the Anglo-Boer War and tribal Africans still use it as a lubricant for women in childbirth.

362. *Dicerocaryum eriocarpum:* Devil's thorn, Beesdubbeltjie

361. *Ceratotheca triloba:* Wild foxglove, Vingerhoedblom

GESNERIACEAE (STREPTOCARPUS)

Streptocarpus is the only genus of the Gloxinia family that is found in South Africa. Some 45 species occur in our region, mainly in cool, moist, forested parts of the South Eastern Cape Province, KwaZulu-Natal, the Northern Province and Mpumalanga. Nearly all these plants are strikingly beautiful and are much admired as house plants. Species like *Streptocarpus rexii* and *Streptocarpus primulifolius* have been extensively used in hybridization programmes to produce more robust floriferous forms. Consequently most of these hybrids sold both in South Africa and abroad are rather different from their first cousins in the KwaZulu-Natal Midlands.

S. vandeleurii and several related species are remarkable in that instead of having a rosette of leaves, they have a single, enormous, rather succulent leaf which supports the entire plant, including a large cluster of tubular, cream-coloured flowers produced in summer.

363. *Streptocarpus vandeleurii*: Olifantsoor

364. *Streptocarpus primulifolius*

SELAGINACEAE

Some botanists prefer to regard the Selaginaceae as a tribe of the Scrophulariaceae, yet it is in fact a distinct family in which there is a single ovule in each chamber of the ovary instead of several ovules as in true Scrophulariaceae. Most are annuals or soft-wooded perennials. The Selaginaceae is almost exclusively confined to Southern Africa where 11 different genera are found with *Selago* the largest, consisting of over 100 species. Several selagos, especially *S. spuria* and *S. serrata*, are exceedingly handsome perennials producing large pinkish to mauve (sometimes white) flowerheads in late spring. At this stage they are little known in gardens but can be expected to generate great interest when eventually introduced into cultivation.

365. *Selago spuria*: Blouaarbossie

366. *Selago spuria*: Blouaarbossie

ACANTHACEAE

The Acanthus family is a large, cosmopolitan group of plants, found in most parts of South Africa except the Western Cape Province. Non-botanists find the Acanthaceae confusingly similar to other related families, yet characteristic explosive seed capsules and distinctive sculpturing on their pollen grains make them readily recognizable. Many such as *Blepharis*, a genus typical of the arid western parts of the country, have spiny leaves.

Shrubby and herbaceous species of *Barleria* are becoming popular garden plants. The autumn-flowering *Barleria obtusa* is often used by gardeners as a ground cover, especially in roadside and embankment plantings. Decoctions of the roots of several other *Barleria* species are used by certain African tribes as a traditional remedy for toothache.

Of the more woody representatives, *Mackaya bella*, a forest undershrub from KwaZulu-Natal, takes well to formal clipping and will flower splendidly in the gloomiest part of a garden where little else will thrive. However, *Ruspolia hypocrateriformis* is not found south of the Soutpansberg: it requires truly sub-tropical conditions to be cultivated successfully.

368. *Crossandra greenstockii*

367. *Blepharis subvolubilis*

370. *Ruspolia hypocrateriformis*

369. *Barleria gueinzii*

371. *Mackaya bella:* Forest bell bush, Bosklokkiesbos

BIGNONIACEAE

South Africa boasts some exceptional members of this largely tropical family. The sausage tree, *Kigelia africana*, could hardly be more appropriately named, yet its singular fruits – which seem to have come straight from a delicatessen's counter – have no gastronomic value. The fruits can in fact be poisonous to man, especially when they are immature, although wild animals are known to eat them. They develop slowly after the rather lurid pendulous blooms have been pollinated. This extraordinary tree grows in the Lowveld in Mpumalanga, KwaZulu-Natal and Swaziland. *Tecomaria capensis*, the Cape honeysuckle, whose honey-filled tubular flowers are such an attraction to sunbirds, is a prominent feature of the Eastern Cape Province although its range extends to KwaZulu-Natal and Mpumalanga. An abundance of blooms in orange, yellow and salmon-pink, and a multiple-stemmed growth habit amenable to clipping and shaping have ensured its popularity as a hedge plant.

On the other hand, *Podranea brycei*, commonly called Zimbabwe creeper, is a robust climber liberally festooned with trusses of pink flowers throughout the summer. Too rampant for the average

372. *Kigelia africana:* Sausage tree, Worsboom

373. *Kigelia africana:* Sausage tree, Worsboom

gardener, it is nevertheless ideal for those who garden on a grand scale. *Rhigozum obovatum*, the yellow pomegranate, is a spare twiggy shrub and is one of the few members of this family that has adapted to arid habitats, such as the central Karoo and parts of the Eastern Cape Province. For much of the year it looks quite dead, but in spring even the most withered branches come to life when the golden yellow blossoms make their brief, brilliant show.

374. *Tecomaria capensis:* Cape honeysuckle, Trompetters

375 *Podranea brycei:* Zimbabwe creeper

376. *Tecomaria capensis:* Cape honeysuckle, Trompetters

377. *Rhigozum obovatum:* Yellow pomegranate, Berggranaat

RUBIACEAE

Gardenias are probably the most familiar members of this huge cosmopolitan family: at least six species are indigenous to South Africa. The much cultivated *Gardenia thunbergia* ranges from the Eastern Cape Province to KwaZulu-Natal. At the end of summer its large, white, deliciously scented blooms are followed by eight centimetre-long oval fruits, hard and woody in texture, which may remain attached to the parent plant for years without releasing their seed. It is believed that these fruits are browsed by kudu or other large ungulates and that their passage through the animal's digestive tract triggers the seeds which then germinate in a bed of dung.

Rothmannia, a related genus of beautiful, white-flowered evergreen trees, bears fruits which are much favoured by wild animals such as monkeys and baboons.

Pavetta, with about 40 species from the Eastern Cape Province, KwaZulu-Natal and Mpumalanga, is also noted for its white, perfumed blooms, but the individual flowers are tightly clustered instead of being produced singly: moreover, they have slender delicate styles protruding from each flower.

Burchellia bubalina, or wild pomegranate, is scentless but produces copious nectar. Birds sometimes tear open the tubular flowers to get at the nectar with such determination that the Zulu people have devised for this tree a far more appropriate name, meaning birds' liquor. The only herbaceous member of the Rubiaceae shown here is *Pentanisia prunelloides*, a blue-flowered grassland herb common in most summer rainfall areas. An infusion of its roots is used by several African tribes for treating venereal diseases.

378. *Hyperacanthus amoenus:* Thorny gardenia, Doringkatjiepiering

379. *Burchellia bubalina:* Wild pomegranate Wildegranaat

380. *Rothmannia globosa:* Bell gardenia, Klokkieskatjiepiering

382. *Gardenia thunbergia:* White gardenia, Witkatjiepiering

31. *Pavetta gracilifolia*

383. *Rothmannia capensis:* Wild gardenia, Wildekatjiepiering

384. *Pentanisia prunelloides:* Wild verbena

ASTERACEAE (COMPOSITAE)

The Asteraceae (alternatively called Compositae) is known to everyone as the daisy family. Comprising some 25 000 species distributed throughout the world, it is one of the largest families of flowering plants. They are considered advanced in evolutionary terms and are certainly one of the most successful plant groups, having adapted to almost every ecological niche and assumed almost every growth form imaginable. Well over 2 000 species are found in South Africa. An important family feature is that each so-called daisy blossom is actually a compound flower-head, usually comprised of numerous tiny individual flowers encircled by brightly coloured rays.

Many members of this family are important ornamentals such as gerberas, the most widely cultivated of our native daisies. Modern *Gerbera* hybrids are mainly derived from *Gerbera jamesonii*, the Barberton daisy of Mpumalanga, and *Gerbera aurantiaca*, the Hilton daisy from central KwaZulu-Natal.

For most South Africans spring at the Cape would be inconceivable without well-known and much loved daisies like *Didelta carnosa* which so often features in the foreground of idyllic picture postcard views of Table Mountain, together with other dune species like *Senecia arenarius* and *Senecia littoreus*.

385. *Didelta carnosa*

Everlastings is a general term for various species of *Helichrysum*, *Syncarpha* and *Phaenocoma*, whose dry papery rays persist, retaining their colour for years; they are collected from the veld in great quantities for dry arrangements. In the Southern Cape districts of Elim and Bredasdorp, *Syncarpha vestita* once formed the basis of an unusual local industry. Detached heads of this aromatic white-flowered everlasting were plucked, dried and then used for stuffing pillows, from whose pungent, herbal petal filling it was claimed that asthmatic sleepers derived considerable relief.

Daisies are so ubiquitous that they are considered common, yet some species like *Senecio coleophyllus*, a tall swamp dweller from the Cape Hangklip Mountains, are exceedingly rare. Others such as *Mairea coriacea* only flower immediately after a veld fire and so at other times are passed unnoticed.

Gazania, *Gorteria*, *Dimorphotheca*, *Felicia*, *Senecio* and *Ursinia* all contribute to the famed spring daisy displays in Namaqualand. They are mostly annuals germinating in response to early autumn rains, growing throughout winter and then flowering in spring,

388. *Felicia amoena*

386. *Gerbera aurantiaca:* Hilton daisy

387. *Senecio arenarius* (purple): Hongerblom

389. *Edmondia sesamoides:* Everlasting, Sewejaartjie

390. *Senecio tamoides*

393. *Senecio coleophyllus*

391. *Gazania krebsiana:* Oranjegousblom

394. *Dimorphotheca cuneata:* Gousblom

392. *Syncarpha vestita:*
Cape everlasting, Sewejaartjie

395. *Phaenocoma prolifera:* Cape everlasting, Rooisewejaartjie

after which they rapidly set seed and die as summer advances. Not every year sees carpets of daisies in Namaqualand, for the volume and regularity of winter rainfall determines the extent of the show: weather conditions in this area are so erratic that one can rarely expect a bumper season more than once a decade.

Another colourful genus in semi-arid regions is *Euryops*, commonly called 'harpuisbos' because of resinous exudations from both stems and leaves. Comprising quick-growing evergreen shrubs, some species such as *E. speciosissimus*, the Clanwilliam daisy, have become popular garden ornamentals.

396. *Gorteria diffusa* subspecies *calendulacea*

398. *Mairea coriacea*

397. *Syncarpha eximia:* Cape everlasting, Rooisewejaartjie

399. *Euryops brevilobus*

400. *Ursinia anthemoides:* Marigold, Bergmargriet

401. *Oldenburgia grandis:*
Suurberg cushion bush, Suurbergse kussingbos

402. *Syncarpha canescens:*
Everlasting, Rooisewejaartjie

403. *Dicoma zeyheri:* Maagwortel

104. *Felicia filifolia:* Draaibossie

Woody, perennial species tend to predominate in the moister eastern half of the country. Several are creepers like *Senecio tamoides*, a yellow winter-flowering species which grows wild near Humansdorp. Around Grahamstown, *Oldenburgia grandis* develops into a most arresting small tree, which produces gigantic thistle-like flowerheads on metre-long stems.

105. *Helichrysum ecklonis*

BIBLIOGRAPHY

The following reference works will provide detailed information on specific aspects of South Africa's wild flowers.

Please note: Not all the publications that are listed below are currently in print.

SOUTHERN AFRICA

Adams, J. (1976). *Wild Flowers of the Northern Cape*, Dept. of Nature and Environmental Conservation, Cape Provincial Administration.

Arnold, T.H. & De Wet, B.C. (1993). *Plants of Southern Africa: names and distribution*, National Botanical Institute, Private Bag X101, Pretoria. (Provides a complete list of plant species indigenous to Southern Africa with recent synonyms and distribution by province.)

Batten, A. & Bokelmann, H. (1966). *Wild Flowers of the Eastern Cape Province*, Books of Africa, Cape Town.

Burman, Lee and Bean, Anne (1985). *Hottentots Holland to Hermanus*, South African Wild Flower Guide No. 5, Botanical Society of South Africa, Kirstenbosch.

Fabian, Anita & Germishuizen, Gerrit (1982). *Transvaal Wild Flowers*, Macmillan, Johannesburg.

Furston, Malcolm (1993). *Bushveld Trees: Lifeblood of the Transvaal Lowveld*, Fernwood Press, Cape Town.

Gibson, J.M. (1975). *Wild Flowers of Natal (coastal region)*, Trustees of the Natal Publishing Trust Fund, Durban.

Gibson, J.M. (1978). *Wild Flowers of Natal (inland region)*, Trustees of the Natal Publishing Trust Fund, Durban.

Gledhill, E. (1969). *Eastern Cape Veld Flowers*, Department of Nature and Environmental Conservation, Cape Provincial Administration.

Hilliard, O.M. and Burtt, B.L. (1987). *The Botany of the Southern Drakensberg*, National Botanic Gardens, Kirstenbosch.

Hobson, N.K., Jessop, J.P., Ginn, M.C. & Kelly, J. (1975). *Veld Plants of Southern Africa* (mainly Karoo region), Macmillan, Johannesburg.

Jeppe, B. (1975). *Natal Wild Flowers*, Purnell & Sons, Johannesburg.

Kidd, Mary Maytham (1983). *Cape Peninsula*, South African Wild Flower Guide No. 3, Botanical Society of South Africa, Kirstenbosch.

Killick, Donald (1990). *A Field Guide to the Flora of the Natal Drakensberg*, Jonathan Ball and Ad. Donker, Johannesburg.

Le Roux, Annelise & Schelpe, Ted (1988). *Namaqualand*, South African Wild Flower Guide No. 1, Botanical Society of South Africa, Kirstenbosch.

Letty, C. (1962). *Wild Flowers of the Transvaal*, Trustees Wildflowers of the Transvaal Book Fund, Pretoria.

Mason, H. (1972). *Western Cape Sandveld Flowers*, C. Struik, Cape Town.

Moriarty, Audrey (1982). *Outeniqua, Tsitsikamma and Eastern Little Karoo*, South African Wild Flower Guide No. 2, Botanical Society of South Africa, Kirstenbosch.

Onderstal, Jo (1984). *Transvaal Lowveld and Escarpment*, South African Wild Flower Guide No. 4, Botanical Society of South Africa, Kirstenbosch.

Pearse, R.O. (1978). *Mountain Splendour: The Wild Flowers of the Drakensberg*, Howard Timmins, Cape Town.

Trauseld, W.P. (1969). *Wild Flowers of the Natal Drakensberg*, Purnell & Sons, Johannesburg.

Van Wyk, P. (1972 and 1974). *Trees of the Kruger National Park* (vols. 1 & 2) Purnell & Sons, Johannesburg.

Van Wyk, Braam and Malan, Sasa (1988). *Field Guide to the Wild Flowers of the Witwatersrand and Pretoria Region*, Struik Publishers, Cape Town.

ALLIED TOPICS OF INTEREST

TREES (GENERAL)

Coates Palgrave, P. (1995). *Trees of Southern Africa*, C. Struik, Cape Town.

Palmer, E. & Pitman, N. (1973). *Trees of Southern Africa* (3 vols.) A.A. Balkema, Cape Town.

VELD TYPES

Acocks, J.P.H. (1988). *Veld Types of South Africa* (3rd ed.) Botanical Research Institute, Pretoria. (Obtainable from National Botanical Institute, Private Bag X101, Pretoria.)

FOLKLORE AND MEDICINAL USES

Fox, W.F. and Norwood Young, M.E. (1982). *Food from the veld. Edible wild plants of Southern Africa botanically identified and described*, Delta Books, Johannesburg.

Smith, C.A. (1966). *Common Names of South African Plants*, Botanical Survey Memoir No. 35, Agricultural Technical Services, Pretoria.

Vahrmeijer, J. (1981). *Poisonous Plants of Southern Africa that cause stock losses*, Tafelberg, Cape Town.

Watt, J.M. & Breyer-Brandwijk, M.G. (1962). *Medicinal and Poisonous Plants of Southern and Eastern Africa* (2nd ed.) E.S. Livingstone, Edinburgh and London.

DETAILED PUBLICATIONS

ASCLEPIADACEAE

White, A. & Sloane, B.L. (1937). *The Stapeliae* (3 vols.) Abbey Garden Press, Pasadena, California.

ERICACEAE

Baker, H.A. & Oliver, E.G. (1967). *Ericas in Southern Africa*, Purnell & Sons, Johannesburg.

Schumann, D. and Kirsten, G. (1992). *Ericas of Southern Africa*, Fernwood Press, Cape Town.

EUPHORBIACEAE

White, A., Dyer, R.A. & Sloane, B.L. (1941). *The Succulent Euphorbiaceae* (2 vols.) Abbey Garden Press, Pasadena, California.

FABACEAE

Carr, J.D. (1976). *The South African Acacias*, Conservation Press, Johannesburg.

Hennesy, E.F. (1972). *South African Erythrinas*, Natal Branch of the Wildlife Protection Society, Durban.

GERANIACEAE

Van der Walt, J.J.A. (1977). *Pelargoniums of Southern Africa*, illus. by Ellaphie Ward-Hilhorst, Purnell & Sons, Johannesburg.

Van der Walt, J.J.A. and Vorster, P.J. (1981). *Pelargoniums of Southern Africa* (Vol. 2) Juta, Cape Town.

Van der Walt, J.J.A. & Vorster, P.J. (1988). *Pelargoniums of Southern Africa*, National Botanic Gardens, Kirstenbosch.

GESNERIACEAE

Hilliard, O.M. & Burtt, B.L. (1971). *Streptocarpus: An African Plant Study*, Natal University Press, Pietermaritzburg.

IRIDACEAE

Goldblatt, P. (1986). *The Moraeas of Southern Africa*, Annals of Kirstenbosch Botanic Garden Vol. 14.

Goldblatt, P. (1989). *The genus Watsonia*, Annals of Kirstenbosch Botanic Garden Vol. 19.

LILIACEAE

Bornman, H. & Hardy, D. (1971). *Aloes of South African Veld*, Voortrekker Pers, Johannesburg.

Duncan, G.D. (1988). *The Lachenalia Handbook*, National Botanic Gardens, Kirstenbosch.

Jeppe, B. (1969). *South African Aloes*, Purnell & Sons, Johannesburg.

Reynolds, G.W. (1950). *Aloes of South Africa*, Aloes of South Africa Book Fund, Johannesburg.

MESEMBRYANTHEMACEAE

Cole, D.T. (1988). *Lithops, flowering stones*, Acorn Books, Randburg.

Herre, H. (1971). *The Genera of the Mesembryanthemaceae*, Tafelberg, Cape Town.

ORCHIDACEAE

Harrison, E.R. (1972). *Epiphytic Orchids of Southern Africa*, KwaZulu-Natal Branch of the Wildlife Protection Society, Durban.

Stewart, J., Linder, H.P., Schelpe, E. and Hall, A.V. (1982). *Wild Orchids of Southern Africa*, Macmillan, Johannesburg.

PROTEACEAE

Rourke, J.P. (1980). *The Proteas of Southern Africa*, Purnell & Sons, Johannesburg.

Vogts, M.M. and Paterson-Jones, C. (1982). *South Africa's Proteaceae, Know them and grow them*, Struik Publishers, Cape Town.

SUCCULENTS

Court, Doreen (1981). *Succulent Flora of Southern Africa*. A comprehensive and authoritative guide to 164 genera in nine family groups. A.A. Balkema, Cape Town.

BULBS

Du Plessis, Neil and Duncan, Graham (1989). *Bulbous Plants of Southern Africa*, (Illustrated by Elise Bodley) Tafelberg, Cape Town.

Jeppe, Barbara (1989). *Spring and winter flowering bulbs of the Cape*, Oxford University Press, Cape Town.

CYCADS

Good, Douglas (1989). *Cycads of Africa*, Struik Winchester, Cape Town.

PHOTOGRAPHIC CREDITS

A. Bannister 1, 7, 36, 136, 186, 273, 294, 334 *M. Bayer* 158, 165 *H. Cameron* 88, 384 *V. Carruthers* 79, 157, 235, 242, 383 *S. Chater* 16, 19, 38, 51, 55, 92, 115, 194, 244, 245, 248, 265, 297, 340, 397, 402 *G. Cubitt* 10, 13, 17, 18, 20, 34, 44, 61, 64, 77, 81, 94, 95, 98, 142, 146, 176, 188, 191, 192, 193, 202, 230, 231, 232, 246, 249, 250, 261, 277, 281, 282, 289, 300, 320, 325, 348, 349, 376, 377, 385, 387, 392, 405 *D. D'Ewes* 33, 330 *O. Dose* 53, 56 *G. Dreyer* half-title page, page opposite title page, pp. 4, 5, 7, 8 *J. Dumoulin* 224, 225, 226 *S. Eliovsen* 40, 86, 253, 371, 390 *A. Elliott* 163, 169, 205 *J. Exelby* 219 *C. Giddy* 5, 9, 12, 21, 22, 24, 28, 48, 76, 78, 172, 187, 190, 195, 222, 228, 229, 241, 279, 284, 313, 324, 333, 344, 351, 357, 372, 380, 386, 396, 400 *H. Hall* 27, 207, 227 *D. Hardy* 280, 319 *H. Harmer* 160, 164, 166, 168, 170, 223 *O. Hilliard* 363 *W. Jackson* 2, 41, 66, 68, p. 121, 126, 128, 143, 155, 171, 173, 179, 204, 220, 267, 268, 272, 274, 275, 276, 295, 298, 304, 305, 306, 307, 338, 342, 353, 364, 393 *N. Jacobson* 378 *E. Lastovica* 62, 72, 97, 133, 189, 206, 211, 236, 238, 264, 287, 309, 365, 401, 403 *F. le Roux* 73, 102, 111, 120 *E. Moll* 151, 278, 283, 358 *J. Morris* 26, 32, 288, 315, 346 *C. Oberholzer* 87 *J. Onderstal* contents page, 11, 15, 99, 100, 101, 141, 156, 239, 243, 255, 262, 263, 285, 290, 360, 361, 362, 373, 379, 381 *R. Pearse* 23, 35, 43, 50, 59, 65, 85, 257, 404 *D. Plowes* 31, 54, 75, 80, 91, 131, 134, 135, 139, 148, 200, 251, 258, 260, 310, 321, 322, 323, 326, 327, 328, 332, 335, 336, 337, 339, 367, 368, 369, 370 *J. Potgieter* 162 *E. Rosenstrauch* 83, 130, 210, 217, 286, 347, 352, 382 *J. Rourke* 121, 127, 138, 234 *F. Rousseau* 103, 105, 106, 118, 119, 122, 123, 124, 329 *P. Sargeant* 3, 4, 6, 8, 25, 29, 30, 37, 39, 45, 46, 47, 52, 57, 58, 60, 63, 67, 70, 71, 74, 89, 90, 93, 96, 107, 109, 110, 112, 114, 116, 117, 125, 132, 140, 144, 145, 147, 149, 150, 153, 154, 159, 161, 174, 175, 177, 178, 180, 185, 201, 203, 233, 240, 247, 266, 269, 270, 291, 292, 293, 296, 299, 301, 302, 303, 308, 311, 312, 350, 354, 359, 366, 388, 389, 398, 399 *L. Stanton* 84, 182, 184, 237, 252, 254, 331 *D. Steele* 108, 213, 259, 318, 374 *J. van Jaarsveld* 104, 256, 345 *U. van der Spuy* 14, 42, 69, 129, 152, 183, 208, 209, 317, 343, 396 *J. van der Walt* 212, 214, 215, 216, 218, 221 *H. Vergnani* 198 *J. Watcham* 49, 82, 113, p. 127, 137, 167, 181, 196, 197, 199, 271, 314, 316, 341, 355, 356, 375, 394, 395.

INDEX